D0362457

Radical Renewal:
The Problem of Wineskins Today

Howard A. Snyder

Radical Renewal:

The Problem of Wineskins Today

TOUCH PUBLICATIONS
P.O. Box 19888 • Houston, TX 77224

PUBLISHED BY TOUCH PUBLICATIONS
HOUSTON, TEXAS

Copyright © 1996 by Howard A. Snyder
All rights reserved. No portion of this book may be reproduced,
stored in a retrieval system, or transmitted in any form or by any
means—electronic, mechanical, photocopy, recording or
otherwise, without the prior written consent of the publisher.

ISBN No. 1-880828-97-9

Unless otherwise indicated, all Scripture quotations used in this book
are from the New Revised Standard Version (NRSV) of the Bible,
and are used by permission.

Scripture quotations, marked (NEB) are from the New English Bible,
copyright © by the delegates of the Oxford University Press and the
Syndics of the Cambridge University Press, 1961, 1970.
Used by permission.

Editing, book layout, cover design and illustration:
Randall Neighbour, Jim Egli, and Rick Chandler.

TOUCH Publications is the book-publishing division of TOUCH
Outreach Ministries, a resource and consulting ministry for churches
with a vision for cell-based local church structure.

Available from:
TOUCH Outreach Ministries
P.O. Box 19888 • Houston, TX USA 77079
Telephone 1-713-497-7901 • Fax 1-713-497-0904

TOUCH International South Africa
Corner Memel & Gemsbok Roads • P.O. Box 1223
Newcastle, South Africa, 2940
Tel. 03431-28126 • Fax 03431-24211

In memory of my parents
Edmund C. Snyder
Clara Zahniser Snyder
who first taught me to love the church

CONCORDIA UNIVERSITY LIBRARY
PORTLAND, OR 97211

Contents

Introduction: New Wine and Old Wineskins

A TIME FOR NEW WINE

1	The Impossible Cataclysm	23
2	World on the Brink?	27
3	The Gospel to the Poor	37

A NEW LOOK AT OLD WINESKINS

4	Churches, Temples, and Tabernacles	55
5	Are Church Buildings Superfluous?	65
6	Must Pastors Be Superstars?	75

BIBLICAL MATERIAL FOR NEW WINESKINS

7	The Fellowship of the Holy Spirit	83
8	The People of God	93
9	The Mind of Christ	103
10	The Ecology of the Church	117
11	The Place of Spiritual Gifts	139
12	The Small Group as Basic Structure	149

CHURCH STRUCTURE IN SPACE AND TIME

13	Church and Culture	161
14	A Lesson From History	179
15	A Look to the Future	187
	Postscript: Parable of the River	199
	Notes	203
	Index	217

Preface

A SMALL ROOT in the right place can crack a whole building. A fine wine of the right brew can burst an old wineskin.

It's the principle of life; of ferment; of small beginnings with great promise.

Radical renewal means getting back to basics; going to the root *(radix)*. Radical renewal is so powerful that it can turn a world rightside up.

But only if the root is alive. Only if the wine is real.

This is a book about radical renewal and the problem of wineskins. Radical renewal is what the church needs most today. As communities claiming the name Christian we must get back to the root; rediscover the gospel wine. And that means a fresh look at wineskins.

This book is a revision and updating of *The Problem of Wineskins,* first published in 1975. Here is why:

At a conference in Korea in 1995, two young pastors from Finland approached me. After introducing themselves the older one said, "I read *The Problem of Wineskins* while I was a seminary student in Sweden. It was very important to me in my training, and has really helped me as a pastor."

That was a great surprise. But I've had similar experiences. The most gratifying thing to me about *Wineskins* has been its impact on young leaders in North America and around the world. The most common reaction I get is that the book helped readers see the church in a new light, tracing a model that is powerful, practical, and biblically sound.

Most of *The Problem of Wineskins* was written while I was living in Brazil. It was a path-finding project for me. The Bible study, research, writing, questions, discussions, prayer, and ministry that gave rise to the book yielded rich fruit. It brought a deepened faith and a renewed hope for the church in the world—for the church *and* the world.

Working through the biblical material on the church (in both Testaments), and especially the book of Ephesians, a whole new understanding opened to me. I began to sense what the early Christians must have felt when they said "church" or "fellowship" or "community." That this was a *new* discovery is, of course, evidence of how largely the biblical concept (or better, *reality*) of the church has been lost in most of traditional Christianity. Fortunately, things are changing!

Leaving the North American scene and ministering in another culture prompted a fundamental rethinking of the mission and structure of the church in today's world. It was my experience of growing up in the church, pastoring in Detroit, and ministering in Brazil that raised the questions. But it was primarily Scripture that gave the answers.

That was over twenty years ago; the turbulent days of the early Seventies. *Wineskins* stayed in print for two decades, and was translated into several languages. Though still in print in some languages, it finally went out of print in the United States.

Since the book was no longer available in English, TOUCH Outreach Ministries offered to reprint it in this revised and updated form. The hope of publisher and author is that a new generation of church leaders will discover the awesome, winsome power of the New Testament church through this and a growing chorus of similar books. Not surprisingly, when we take the biblical witness on its own terms instead of importing our preconceptions and misconceptions into it, a consensus emerges as to the basic nature of the Christ's Body. Thus many books today point in the same general direction.

The changes in this reworked edition of *Wineskins* mainly have to do with global cultural shifts over the past two decades. But I have made a number of other changes for greater clarity and sharpness. The biggest change is the addition of a whole new chapter, "The Ecology of the Church," included here as chapter 10. This was the key chapter in my 1983 book *Liberating the Church* (now out of print). Because this chapter develops further some of the insights in *Wineskins* and presents a practical organic model of church life, I believe it greatly strengthens the book to include it here. I have also added a postscript.

This book attempts to restate the biblical view of the church in the light of contemporary culture. While I am perhaps clearer today about the biblical vision of the church, I remain convinced that the argument traced in the original book is biblically sound and amazingly relevant. As to the cultural context, the directions I pointed out twenty years ago seem even more on target today.

My conclusion—firmer today, after broader experience of the global church and contact with many people who have used *Wineskins* in widely varied contexts—is that the biblical model works, if it is worked.

Howard A. Snyder
Dayton, Ohio

Introduction:

New Wine and Old Wineskins

RECENTLY I RECEIVED an e-mail message from my friend Joe Culumber in Seattle. Joe pastors a growing multi-ethnic congregation in the city. He wrote:

> *There are some real dynamics at work in the church here—things are "getting out of hand" in the positive sense. People are taking the initiative and doing ministry without even consulting me! And five or six persons of different ages and gender are considering moving in the direction of "full-time" ministry, which is both exciting and challenging.*

Sounds like a church undergoing radical renewal; solving the problem of wineskins.

Frankly, I have never had much experience with either wine or wineskins—of the literal variety. But Jesus' words in Luke 5:37-38 have long intrigued me: "No one puts new wine into old wineskins, for the new wine bursts the old skins, ruining the skins and spilling the wine. New wine must be put into new wineskins" (Living Bible).

What did Jesus mean? Certainly he did not mean everything that Christians through the ages have taken from these words. Jesus distinguishes here between something essential and primary (the wine) and something secondary but also necessary and useful (the wineskins). Wineskins would be superfluous without the wine.

This distinction is vital for the everyday life of the church. There is that which is new, potent, essential—the gospel of Jesus

Christ. And there is that which is secondary, subsidiary, made by human hands. These are the wineskins—traditions, structures and patterns of doing things that have grown up around the gospel.

I am particularly concerned here with the *relationship* between such wineskins and the gospel wine. *What kinds of wineskins* are most compatible with the gospel in our emerging global society? For the wineskins are the point of contact between the wine and the world. They are determined both by the wine's properties and the world's pressures. Wineskins result when the divine gospel touches human culture.

In the passage about wineskins in Luke 5, Jesus' critics pose a question: "John's disciples, like the disciples of the Pharisees, frequently fast and pray, but your disciples eat and drink."

Jesus first answers by speaking of the bridegroom. "You cannot make wedding guests fast while the bridegroom is with them, can you? The days will come when the bridegroom will be taken away from them, and then they will fast in those days." Jesus himself was the bridegroom, and while he was on earth with his disciples it was entirely appropriate for them to feast and celebrate.

But Jesus does not stop there. He goes on to speak of new cloth and new wine. Jesus knew where the real problem was. He knew what was behind the question raised by the scribes and Pharisees. They were irked because Jesus was not obeying their traditions. They were really asking the same question they had raised in Matthew 15:2: "Why do your disciples break the tradition of the elders?"

So Jesus says, "No one tears a piece from a new garment and sews it on an old garment; otherwise the new will be torn, and the piece from the new will not match the old. And no one puts new wine into old wineskins; otherwise the new wine will burst the skins and will be spilled, and the skins will be destroyed. But new wine must be put into fresh wineskins."

The last statement is the key: "New wine must be put into fresh wineskins." Good old Judaism could not contain the new wine of Christ. The Christian faith would have to grow and burst the old wineskins. And it happened. The church began to spread into the whole world, shedding the old Jewish forms.

A Message of Newness

We learn two things here. First, this parable reminds us that God is always a God of *newness.* The gospel is new—always.

The Old Testament frequently speaks of new things. We read of a new song, a new heart, a new spirit, a new name, a new covenant, a new creation, a new heaven and a new earth.[1] David said, "He put a new song in my mouth" (Psalms 40:3). And we read other statements such as these:

"See, the former things have come to pass, and new things I now declare; before they spring forth, I tell you of them" (Isaiah 42:9).

"I am about to do a new thing; now it springs forth, do you not perceive it?" (Isaiah 43:19).

"I will give them one heart, and put a new spirit within them" (Ezekiel 11:19).

"For I am about to create new heavens and a new earth" (Isaiah 65:17).

The *New* Testament paints a similar picture in telling the gospel story. Hebrews 10:20 speaks of "the new and living way." And Jesus said on that terrible Last Supper night, "This is my blood of the new covenant" (Matthew 26:28).

God is a God of newness. On the one hand God is the Ancient of Days, "the Father of lights, with whom there is no variation or shadow due to change" (James 1:17). Jesus Christ is "the same yesterday and today and forever" (Hebrews 13:8). But this does not mean that God is static or stationary. The story of God's people in the Bible and the history of the Christian church show just the opposite. In every age the true biblical gospel is a message of newness, of radical renewal.

God has not stopped doing new things. The Bible says, "We wait for new heavens and a new earth where righteousness is at home" (2 Peter 3:13). Many of the Old Testament prophecies about "new things" were fulfilled in part with the coming of Christ and the birth of the church, the new community. But the prophetic fund has not been exhausted. Unfulfilled prophecies and untapped promises of new things remain. At the end of the Bible God is still saying, "See, I am making all things new"! (Revelation 21:5).

Every age tastes the temptation to forget that the gospel is ever new. We try to contain the new wine of the gospel in old wine-skins—outmoded traditions, obsolete philosophies, creaking institutions, old habits. But with time the old wineskins begin to bind the gospel. Then they must burst, and the power of the gospel pours forth once more.

Many times this has happened in the history of the church. Human nature wants to conserve, but the divine nature is to renew. It seems almost a law that things initially created to aid the gospel eventually become obstacles—old wineskins. Then God has to smash or desert them so that the gospel wine can refresh our world once again.

The gospel is new in our day. It is still "the power of God." It is still bursting old wineskins and flowing forth into the world. In fact this is more true today, and in more places, than any time in history. All I attempt to say in this book grows out of a deep confidence in Jesus Christ and in the renewing power of his gospel.

But there is something else this parable teaches us: the *necessity* of new wineskins. Wineskins are not eternal; not sacred. As time passes they must be replaced—not because the gospel changes, but because the gospel itself demands and produces change! New wine must be put into new wineskins—not once-for-all, but repeatedly, periodically. This book is written to accent the *relativity of church structures* and to suggest starting points for the necessary updating of wineskins.

Six New Currents

In writing this book I have been influenced by many renewal currents and movements. In the original edition I mentioned four streams that were stirring the church in the early Seventies: personal evangelism, church renewal, church growth, and the Charismatic Movement. Today much has changed, though one can trace lines of connection over the past quarter-century. Globally, the big story is the remarkable growth of the Christian Church in hundreds of people groups around the world over the past three decades.

More recently, six new movements have emerged. To some degree they grew out of the ferment of the Seventies, and they all confirm aspects of the biblical dynamic of the church, as traced in this book.

1. The movement of *base Christian communities* or *comunidades de base,* especially among Roman Catholics in Latin America, began in the early 1970s and continues, with many mutations. These

"grass-roots communities" apparently number in the hundreds of thousands, and most are poor, accenting the themes of chapter 3 in this book.[2]

2. An expanding and very diverse *house church movement* is showing the viability and continued attractiveness of fairly unstructured, low-profile, face-to-face churches in widely different cultural contexts. The house church movement in China is the largest and most dynamic example, but informal networks of house churches of different kinds are now found in many countries of the world.[3]

3. The *cell church movement* has caught on as a specific way of being and doing church, and is now international in its reach. This movement demonstrates conclusively the power of small, committed circles of believers and the thirst of many people for specific commitment and discipleship.[4]

4. The *meta-church movement* is becoming the dynamic model of many large Protestant churches in the United States and elsewhere. Its key insights are the importance of small groups as structures for discipling and ministry development and the ministry of all believers.[5] We see the obvious impact of megachurches, but only megachurches that follow the meta-church model will remain biblically dynamic.

5. Today there is a also growing *prayer movement* in many places, with roots primarily in Korea and North America. Though this movement does not specifically stress new wineskins, it is opening people to hear the Spirit's whisper and bringing Christians together in a prayerful experience of church.[6]

6. Finally and more generally, we may mention the so-called *Third Wave* of the Pentecostal-Charismatic movement with its continuing emphasis on the gifts and power of the Spirit. Statistically, most Christians in the world today are Charismatic Christians—a dramatic change in the past quarter-century. While in some places this "wave" is drifting into sensationalism or sinking into success, in many areas it represents the cutting edge of church growth.[7]

Other currents are emerging which bear watching, and which may interact with the above movements and trends. Promise Keepers rose as a movement in the early 1990s and is bringing many men to a new sense of Christian responsibility and discipleship. It is unclear so far what impact this will have on local churches. But it provides an opportunity for alert churches that know how to channel new spiritual energy into functional wineskins.

Another trend is the emergence of Christians meeting on the Internet, forming what some are calling a global CyberChurch. Many online discussion groups are already active around topics such as house churches, church leadership, Promise Keepers, and so forth. Some see a significant next step: the creation of a Christian cyber-community, a new form of the church that could transcend racial, ethnic, and socioeconomic divisions. No one knows where this will lead, but we should be alert to the promises and the perils.

These various currents are not the focus of this book. It is noteworthy, however, that all of the six currents discussed above accent one or more of the themes discussed in the following pages. The wine was already fermenting in the early Seventies. Today we note these new currents and discern considerable interflow among them.

All these currents, or the impulse behind them, have played some part in this book. But the heart of the book grows out of an ongoing dialogue with the Word of God and with others who, like me, have continued the quest to rediscover the true, biblical church of Jesus Christ.

A Living Organism

The Bible says the church is nothing less than the Body of Christ. It is the Bride of Christ (Revelation 21:9), the living branches (John 15:1-8), the flock of God (1 Peter 5:2), a holy temple in the Lord (Ephesians 2:21-22). All these biblical images emphasize an essential, living, love relationship between Christ and the church. Even the "temple" is alive, a living organism! These figures underscore the overwhelming importance of the church in God's plan and remind us that "Christ loved the church and gave himself up for her" (Ephesians 5:25). If the church is the Body of Christ—the means of the Head's action in the world—than the church is an essential part of the gospel, and ecclesiology is inseparable from soteriology. So we must deal with radical renewal of the wineskins.

The reader will soon discover that I have not attempted to give a complete program for church structure. No detailed blueprint is proposed. Rather, I have tried to speak more basically about key principles and understandings that must shape any valid and biblical structure in our day. The book is suggestive, not definitive. I have opened more doors than I have chosen (or been able) to enter. Several questions are dealt with only partially and incompletely. Others of my books deal with some of these issues more fully—particularly *The Community of the King, Liberating the Church,* and *A Kingdom Manifesto.* Also, more detailed and systematic proposals for church structure can be found in some of the books cited in the notes throughout the book.

New wine must be put into new wineskins. But where do these wineskins come from? Who supplies them? How are they made? What determines their usefulness?

This book seeks to answer such questions.

A Time For New Wine

The Impossible Cataclysm

IT IS HARD to escape the conclusion that one of the greatest roadblocks to the gospel of Jesus Christ today is the institutional church. Some years ago a student protester held up a sign, "Jesus Yes! Christianity No!" I think he expressed what many feel: The institutional church too often represents something radically different from the Jesus Christ of the Bible.

But how can one get at Christ if not through the church? And how can the church show Jesus without itself getting in the way? In our fast-changing world fewer and fewer people are interested in a pile of old wineskins, no matter how well-preserved they are.

The situation today is not without its ironic humor. On the one hand, much of the institutionalized church talks to itself in a corner about how to be relevant and usually comes up with a theology that has as its unstated premise, "If you can't beat 'em, join 'em." Too often it presents a "theology" of political and/or social causes so hopelessly tied to passing cultural fads that its demise precedes that of its promoters.

Meanwhile, back at the TV screen, proliferating talk shows are on center stage, ignoring the church as they blab about their *experiences* and *relationships*. People don't want a theology to believe or even a cause to live for but first of all an experience that feels real. Lacking that, they stuff their lives with the emotional Styrofoam of sex, drugs, self-serving relationships, and New Age mysticism. Teen gangs and even punk rock and rap groups are really acting out a parable. They say, "Give us a taste of experience."

We *could* do this. The church could present Christ, not an

institution or a theology or a program. The church could present Jesus, not an antiquated and adulterated Christianity. But of course it doesn't. It tries to brew new wine instead of scrapping the old wineskins.[1] Too often the church is not only *in* the world; it is, to a large degree, also *of* the world.

I write as an evangelical who accepts the Bible as fully authoritative. If we were talking here only in theological terms, we could aim our criticisms against the church and remain ourselves comfortably undisturbed, for we could attribute all faults to doctrinal liberalism. But when we speak of such matters as class divisions, racial discrimination, institutionalism, neglect of the poor and the inner city, and lack of social conscience and cultural impact, we are confronting problems that are just as present (and sometimes more so) in evangelical and fundamentalist churches as in so-called liberal churches.

Proposals Heretical and Insufficiently Radical

The church today does not lack proposals for renewal, of course. But most of these suggestions are either heretical or insufficiently radical. They are heretical: They scrap the biblical gospel for something more "relevant." Or they are not radical enough: They try to hold on to too much of existing church tradition, organization and structure. Most programs for renewal from evangelical authors fall into the latter category, with a few notable exceptions.

Many Christians know, of course, that Something Is Wrong. Significant books by evangelicals—such as Robert Coleman's little classic, *The Master Plan of Evangelism,* and more recently Charles Colson's *The Body*—attempt to set forth New Testament principles of what the church should be and how it should witness. The problem is that most books don't go far enough. Much writing on New Testament methods of evangelism and discipleship for instance, while useful, attempt to graft New Testament methods into ecclesiastical structures which are decidedly not New Testament in nature. In contrast, many of the books that deal with church growth and church structure neglect the all-important biblical emphasis on costly discipleship and life-changing community. Often suggestions about structure do not take seriously enough the New Testament concept of the church.

24

For a radical gospel (the biblical kind) we need a radical church (the biblical kind). For the ever-new wine we must continually have new wineskins.

In short, we need a cataclysm.

Something could be done. The institutionalism could be stripped away.

What would a denomination or local church do that really wanted to experience the New Testament dynamic? Let us suppose . . .

First, all church buildings are sold. The money is given (literally) to the poor. All congregations of more than two hundred members are divided in two. Store fronts, small halls, or community centers are rented as needed. Sunday school promotion and most publicity are dropped. Believers gather often in private homes; midweek prayer services become superfluous.

Pastors get secular jobs and cease to be paid by the church; they become, in effect, trained "laymen" instead of paid professionals. "Lay" men and women take the lead in all affairs of the church. There is no attempt to attract unbelievers to church services; these are primarily for believers, and perhaps are held at some time other than Sunday morning.

Evangelism takes on new dimensions. The church begins to take seriously its charge to preach the gospel to the poor and be an agent of the kingdom of God. It ceases to take economic potential into consideration in planting new churches. It begins to lose its enchantment with suburban materialism.

Et cetera.

What would happen to such a church? I suggest it would grow—and might very well replay the book of Acts.

This is the needed cataclysm, in general outline if not in specific detail. This cataclysm would bring the church close to the New Testament model and spirit. But it is an impossible cataclysm. No denomination or congregation in its right institutional mind will ever do such a thing, for perfectly good psychological and sociological (if nor biblical) reasons.

Dietrich Bonhoeffer wrote fifty years ago,

The Church is the Church only when it exists for others. To make a start, it should give away all its property to those in need. The

*clergy must live solely on the free-will offerings of their congre-
gations, or possibly engage in some secular calling. The Church
must share in the secular problems of ordinary human life, not
dominating, but helping and serving. It must tell [people] of
every calling what it means to live in Christ, to exist for others.*[2]

This, in essence if not in detail, is the cataclysm we need. But,
unfortunately, it is an impossible one.

Or is it?

Is not God still saying, "I will do a new thing . . ."?

World on the Brink?

THE CHURCH ON the brink of the twenty-first century should take a hard look at the world we are living in.

Half a century ago, Dietrich Bonhoeffer wrote from his Nazi prison cell that the world had "come of age." The phrase echoed through the church for decades. Now it sounds a bit quaint. Today it seems more accurate to say that the world is on the brink of chaos, even as it is more and more linked electronically.[1]

Bonhoeffer had a point, however. And it relates to the question of the church's mission and structure.

Bonhoeffer believed the world had come of age in the sense that the hypothesis of God is no longer needed. People don't need "God" in order to explain the world. This is true, he said, not only in science and philosophy, but now even in religion itself.

Bonhoeffer wrote, "Since Kant [God] has been relegated to a realm beyond the world of experience."[2] Christians must openly accept this new godlessness, he insisted, and in the midst of this new worldview confront people with Christ. Said Bonhoeffer, "We should frankly recognize that the world, and people, have come of age."[3] "The world that has come of age is more godless, and perhaps for that very reason nearer to God, than the world before its coming of age."[4] His concern, he said, was "how to claim for Jesus Christ a world that has come of age."[5]

But how do things look today? Has the world really "come of age," or is it dying of old age? What kind of world *is* this?

It is a world secularized and urbanized, a "seculurban" world. Yet it is also a world where new superstitions rush in where old dogmas feared to tread; a world where city folks can be just as isolated and insulated—and just as parochial—as their rural forebears. The secular city is becoming re-enchanted.

Today's high-tech men and women are facing a failure of nerve. What was heralded as our adulthood, our maturity, our secular confidence, is being undermined by self-doubt. We are in a new age of anxiety.

To what age *have* we come, then? Where are we on the road map of world history?

Rather than having come of age, history has come full circle. It has returned in several key respects to the spirit of the first-century Roman world. And therefore *this age may be the most strategic one for the effective proclamation of the biblical gospel.*

E. M. Blaiklock observed, "Of all the centuries, the twentieth is most like the first: city-ridden, marred by tyranny, decadent, and wracked by those crises that [our] abuse of [one another] and of [our] native earth engenders."[6] A parallel between today's civilization and the first-century world has been suggested by others, as well. Some years ago futurologists Herman Kahn and Anthony Wiener of the Hudson Institute, projecting toward the Year 2000, noted several "parallels between Roman times and ours." They suggested that "some of the prospects for the year 2000 are, in effect, a return to a sort of new Augustinian age."[7] Discussing current culture, they said that "something very much like our multi-fold trend occurred in Hellenistic Greece, the late Roman Republic, and the early Roman Empire."[8]

Kahn and Wiener's "multifold trend" was toward "increasingly sensate, secular, pragmatic cultures; the accumulation and application of scientific and technological knowledge; the increasing tempo and institutionalization of change; and increasing education, urbanization, and affluence."[9] From our perspective on the eve of the year 2000, we can see the accuracy of this projection, though we see also a growing gap between the affluent and the poor of the earth.

Historian Adolf Harnack listed several first-century conditions which especially aided the growth of early Christianity. Parallels with today are striking. Harnack cited "the blending of different nationalities," "the comparative unity of language and ideas," "the practical and theoretical conviction of the essential unity" of humankind and, especially, "the rising vogue of a mystical philosophy of religion with a craving for some form of revelation and a thirst for miracle."[10]

Seven Signs of the Times

A quick check of today's cultural climate compared with that of the first Century Roman Empire does in fact yield several significant parallels.

1. *An essentially urban world with cities playing the leading cultural role.* The urban flavor of the first century emerges clearly in the Book of Acts and in Paul's writings. In contrast to most of the Middle Ages, "the Graeco-Roman world was a congeries of cities," wrote historian Kenneth Latourette.[11] It was the world of Rome, Alexandria, Ephesus, Corinth, Colossae, Thessalonica, Sardis, Philadelphia, Smyrna, Laodicea, Ancyra, Antioch (capital of Syria and third largest city in the empire) and literally hundreds of other cities. Rome, the largest, had a first-century population of possibly one million, and the population of Alexandria has been estimated at 500,000. Many cities apparently numbered in excess of 100,000 (including slaves); we know the stadium at Ephesus could seat 25,000.[12]

Estimates vary for the first-century population of the total Roman Empire, but sixty million seems a reasonable figure. Of this total perhaps as many as ten million, or about 15%, lived in major cities of 100,000 or more. Considering the large number of smaller cities then in existence, perhaps nearly half the population lived in cities—a situation that later changed drastically.

The important fact, however, is not percentages but influence. Regardless of the proportion actually urbanized (by today's standards), it is clear that urban life and culture played the dominant role in the first century. The city was the place to be; the Book of Acts reflects this.

The fact of urbanization today is too well known to need much comment. "By the year 2000, one half of the human race will be living in cities," reports *Cities & Slums News*, and most of these people will be poor. The world now has over 20 cities with populations of one million or more.[13]

Thus one can trace an urban parallel between the Roman Empire and the world today—statistically, but especially culturally. For urbanization is more than quantitative. "The study of the city has become the study of contemporary society," says Leonard Reissman.[14] Harvey Cox notes, "Urbanization means a structure of common life in which diversity and the disintegration of tradition are paramount," where "high mobility, economic concentration, and mass communication have drawn even rural villages into the web of urbanization."[15] Cox thinks this is a uniquely twentieth-century phenomenon, but the first-century parallel is striking.

2. *Unparalleled peace, stability and political unity.* "War is one of the constants of history," wrote the Durants in *The Lessons of History.* "In the last 3421 years of recorded history only 268 have seen no war."[16] Yet the Christian faith burst into the Roman world during a time of unusual peace. Caesar Augustus had stabilized the entire empire, bringing about "a time of peace unparalleled in history."[17]

At first glance today's world does not look very pacific. We think of the Balkans, parts of the former Soviet Union, several nations of central Africa; of political, economic and ethnic strife; crime in the streets, and so on. Yet by contrast with the past, and considering today's lightning social revolutions, the era since 1945 has been remarkably peaceful. Despite local turbulence, the world today demonstrates a surprising overall stability. A major world war seems less likely now than it did just thirty years ago. An international agreement ending war in Bosnia was signed in 1995. And this follows major recent steps toward peace in the Middle East, South Africa, and Northern Ireland.

Certainly no global political unity comparable to the Roman Empire's position in the Mediterranean world exists today. Yet the far-flung American military and economic presence, plus the growth of the United Nations, plus the expanding web of technological advance and the growth of world trade have produced what may be a functional equivalent of the Roman Empire and the *Pax Romana.*

3. *The worldwide spread of one predominant culture and language.* Greek culture dominated the first-century Roman world. Throughout the Empire, even in Italy, Greek was the common second language. Greek ideas were adopted or mimicked in nearly every province. Roman children were taught in Greek.

The parallel with American influence today (for good or ill) is striking. School children from Russia to China study English. The world goes to American movies and adopts American styles. America is still the world's leading exporter of technological, scientific, and especially cultural innovation.

4. *International travel, communication and cultural interchange.* Roman roads (52,000 miles of them, by one estimate[18]) are legendary; their safety and maintenance in the first century find parallel only in our day. Businessmen, government officials, military personnel, scholars and others traveled widely and with ease throughout the empire. Knowledge and communication mushroomed, creating something like today's knowledge explosion. Harnack speaks of "the ubiquitous merchant and soldier—one may add, the ubiquitous professor."[19]

The situation is similar today—but now globally. Never before has travel been so easy, so safe, so comparatively cheap, or so extensive. Business men and women, students, educators, church leaders, tourists, athletes and government personnel travel constantly almost all over the globe. Even China has opened up. Worldwide travel has reached record levels. Cultural exchange, both official and unofficial, goes on apace, often unnoticed.

Then there is the world of modern mass communications—satellites, national and international publications, global television, the wire services, unprecedented book publishing, and now the Internet, interactively linking over 50 million people worldwide. Ours is the communications age. New ideas and styles quickly become the possession of the world. The situation is unparalleled, but on its own scale, the first century was remarkably similar.

5. *Pervasive social change, with a tendency toward a humanizing, universalist, "one world" outlook; a feeling that humanity is essentially one and shares a common destiny.* Any broad movement of people and ideas tends to unravel the fabric of tradition and produce social change. This was true in the days of the early church. Harnack cites Ulhorn's description of the first-century world:

> Ancient life had . . . begun to break up; its solid foundations had begun to weaken. . . . The idea of universal humanity had disengaged itself from that of nationality. The Stoics had passed the word that all [people] were equal, and had spoken of brotherhood as well as the duties of [people toward each other].

Hitherto despised, the lower classes had asserted their position. The treatment of slaves became milder. Women, hitherto without any legal rights, received such in increasing numbers. Children were looked after. The distribution of grain . . . became a sort of poor-relief or welfare system, and we meet with a growing number of generous deeds, gifts, and endowments, which already exhibit a more humane spirit."[20]

This picture fits not only the age of Paul but also, to a surprising degree, our own. Zbigniew Brzezinski wrote in *Between Two Ages,* "We . . . have reached the stage in [human] history where the passion for equality is a universal, self-conscious force. The passion of equality is strong today because for the first time in human history inequality is no longer insulated by time and distance."[21] Scaled down to the times, nearly the same was true of the Roman Empire. The passion for equality was not as great, but it was present and growing. And its essential presupposition, that humankind is basically one, was a powerful molding force then as now.

6. *Widespread religious and philosophical ferment; the mixture and "relativization" of worldviews; the rise of new religions; a practical atheism and disbelief in the gods, coupled with an existential mysticism.* Here we have, spiritually, the most characteristic first-century condition— and the most important one for the Christian Faith. Latourette notes that this "ethical, philosophical, and religious ferment is one of the chief reasons for Christianity's remarkable spread."[22] And it is here the parallel with today is the most impressive.

We should note four more or less distinct first-century trends here. First was a practical atheism resulting from a strong reaction against traditional religion and its gods. Popular writers ridiculed the gods of traditional mythology. "Thoughtful people reflected on the cruelties, adulteries, deceits, battles and lies attributed to the gods, and they were repelled."[23] Many people no longer took traditional religion seriously.

Something similar is happening today. We see growing disenchantment with both ideology and traditional religion, whether in the form of the "collapse of Communism," the abandonment of traditional beliefs in Africa and the Orient, or reaction against institutional Christianity in the West. Belief has become relativized. Ours is "the age of volatile belief"

(Brzezinski), of "the end of ideology" (Daniel Bell), of "relativized worldviews" (Harvey Cox) and a "crisis of cultural authority" (Os Guinness).[24] As Brzezinski notes,

In our time the established ideologies are coming under attack because their institutionalized character, which was once useful in mobilizing the relatively uneducated masses, has become an impediment to intellectual adaptation, while their concern with the external qualities of life is increasingly felt to ignore the inner, more spiritual dimension. Compelling ideologies thus are giving way to compulsive ideas, . . .

Yet there is still a felt need for a synthesis that can define the meaning and the historical thrust of our times.[25]

Second, this religious ferment included the rise of new, intensely emotional religions and the resurgence of some of the older oriental faiths. In the Roman Empire the cults of Cybele, Isis and Mithras (the last imported from Persia) were especially popular, but there were many others. "By the first century A.D. the Graeco-Roman world was inundated with mystery cults of this sort," writes Michael Green, and "the enthusiasm engendered by these cults was great."[26]

This trait also finds many modern parallels: the resurgence of some Buddhist and Hindu sects, the growth of Islam in the West, the phenomenal spread of spiritism in Brazil and elsewhere, and the new religions of Korea and Japan. These and similar movements often exhibit an intense emotional nature in which experience overshadows specific belief.

A related parallel is the popularity of astrology. Green cites "the rise and great popularity of the pseudo-science of astrology in the last century B.C."[27] Today the popularity of astrology continues to grow (it's even on the Internet) and has been recorded in the popular press.[28]

A third aspect of first-century religious ferment was the rise of an irrational mysticism and an emphasis on experience rather than reason. Notes Latourette, "The intellectuals were despairing of the ability of the unaided human mind to arrive at truth."[29] As already noted, Harnack mentions this as one of the "external conditions" of the first-century world.

The situation today looks like a replay of the first century. Different writers have remarked on humanity's "escape from reason." *Experiencing* is the thing, whether through drugs, violence, entertainment, glossolalia or meditation. One has only to look at the mess we are in today, it is said, to see where rationalism leads. Some see a return to romanticism; others say it is really the rise of irrationalism.

A fourth trend showing religious ferment was a general theological and ideological confusion and a quest for new directions. For the first century, this was largely the fruit of rising disbelief in the traditional gods. The popularization of Plato's philosophy and his attacks on the gods left thinkers in a philosophical and theological vacuum. Traditional gods were dead. What was to replace them?

The parallel today is widespread relativism, theological ignorance, and broad questioning of the whole direction of Western thought since Descartes and Kant. The intellectual movement known as Postmodernism, with its watchword of "deconstruction," holds up a mirror to today's cultural confusion. Todd Gitlin writes, "History has ruptured, passions have been expended, belief has become difficult; heroes have died and been replaced by celebrities."[30]

7. *Moral degeneration.* In the 1975 edition of *Wineskins* I wrote, "I add this last parallel with some hesitation, since it has been so often cited and so frequently overworked." But the social decay in North America and elsewhere over the past twenty years erases my hesitation. Politicians and leaders of all stripes now point to the need for "values," even if they aren't sure where to base them. Here also one notes a parallel with the world of the early church. The progressive, predictable exploitation of sex and violence today, often leading directly into homosexuality and sado-masochism, is probably unparalleled since Roman times.

Three Objections

With parallels also come contrasts. Three differences between today and the first century should be noted.

First, our age stands at the end of twenty centuries of Christian history, whereas the first century was a pre-Christian age. Considering this, are these parallels really valid?

While this difference is important, it does not cancel the main point I am making here, for two reasons. One is that Judaism had spread rapidly throughout the Roman world during the four centuries before Christ, both as a religious faith and as a perspective on reality, a worldview. During this time Judaism was an intensely missionary faith.[31] Its leavening influence was somewhat parallel to the role of Christianity today and in past centuries.

The other qualifying factor is Christianity's remarkable self-renewing capacity. Many times at the very moment in history when the visible, institutional church was dying and funeral preparations were underway, the Christian Faith was quietly being reborn in new movements and wineskins which only later became recognized. There are some signs that this is happening today. Christianity may be, *at one and the same time,* one of the old, traditional religions being abandoned and one of the new, dynamic, emerging faiths. The growth of cell churches and other "new" forms of the church in the United States and elsewhere and remarkable Christian growth in Korea and China in recent decades are notable examples.

A second difference is the totally new fact of the computer-electronics revolution. Here there is no real first-century parallel. Yet there is something of a negative parallel. While computerized technology is a new fact, many react against it by turning to irrationalism and mysticism—a response which parallels first-century reaction against contemporary philosophy and science.

The implications of the technological revolution for the Christian faith will be far-reaching and need careful analysis. I will have more to say later about the importance of this revolution for the church.

Finally, the Roman Empire was not really the whole world, but only a restricted part of it, whereas today we think in truly global terms. But this is just the point. We are seeing emerge a situation similar to that of the first-century Roman Empire, *but today on a global scale.* Christianity was born into this Roman world "in the fullness of time" and turned it upside down. May not this happen again in our age—worldwide?

Often we are shocked and dismayed by crime statistics and other indicators of moral decline, or by other signs of today's cultural crisis. But rather than be dismayed, perhaps we should look at these signs in another light. For we as Christians know that the true church of Jesus Christ can never be in any real danger of extinction. Institutionalized religion may decline. Immorality may grow. Oppression and injustice may increase. But even through these things God may be preparing a new revolutionary outbreak of the gospel that will once again alter the course of human history. Christ came "in the fullness of time," when the stage was set. And God is setting the stage today for a great moving of his hand— perhaps the last great moving in world history.

There are encouraging signs—the house church movement in China, increasing reports of revival in many places, widespread new forms of Christian community,[32] unprecedented Christian publishing, rapid church growth among many of the world's people groups, new openness to the gospel among some peoples long thought resistant, new and persuasive voices in fundamental theology, growing cooperation between Evangelicals and Roman Catholics on social and moral issues. It may indeed be that the world is coming of age in the most profound sense—coming to recognize its utter need for a sure word from the living God.

The needed cataclysm in the institutional church still looks impossible. But maybe the overflowing new wine will find new wineskins, catalysts for cataclysm.

Prophecies such as Joel 2:28-32 were not exhausted on the Day of Pentecost. A fund of biblical prophecies remains stored up for our day, and not all of these prophecies speak negatively of judgment.[33] God will yet do a new thing!

> *Then afterward I will pour out my Spirit on all flesh; your sons and your daughters shall prophesy, your old men shall dream dreams, and your young men shall see visions. Even on the male and female slaves, in those days, I will pour out my Spirit. . . . Then everyone who calls on the name of the LORD shall be saved (Joel 2:28-29, 32).*

With the world coming full circle and conditions so strikingly like New Testament days, it is not unreasonable to hope for the emergence of a church with New Testament energy.

Now, a church with New Testament energy is one that preaches the gospel to the poor.

3

The Gospel to the Poor

JESUS CAME PREACHING the gospel to the poor. The Old Testament repeatedly speaks of God's care for the poor, the fatherless, the widow, the oppressed. Radical renewal calls us to hear this biblical concern for the poor, for here we feel the heartbeat of God.

There is loose in the church the strange idea that solid, self-supporting churches cannot be planted among the poor, at least not without heavy subsidies and leadership from richer churches. There is some truth to this—*if* we mean churches modeled after the traditional institutionalized pattern of expensive buildings and bureaucratic organization. But if our concern is to plant New Testament churches, we had better take a second look at the New Testament gospel. And what it says about the poor.

Examining biblical references to the poor several years ago alerted me to God's special concern for the poor. Too often, however the church has neglected this concern—to its own hurt.[1] This issue is tied closely to church structure, as we shall see.

Jesus certainly put no restrictions on the Great Commission. The good news is to be carried to every class and people. Yet by both word and example Jesus shows that the poor have a special place in God's plan. And the entire Bible is remarkably consistent in sounding this theme.

The Poor in the Old Testament

From the Mosaic covenant to the promises of the gospel, the Bible is continually pointing to the poor, the widow, the orphan, the alien, the needy and the oppressed.

The Old Testament reveals several significant facts, surprising

37

facts, about God's attitude toward the poor. We read that the Lord especially loves the poor and does not forget them. God's anointed one "delivers the needy when they call, the poor and those who have no helper. He has pity on the weak and the needy, and saves the lives of the needy" (Ps. 72:12-13). The Lord "does not forget the cry of the afflicted" (Ps. 9:12). God has been a "refuge to the poor, a refuge to the needy in their distress" (Isa. 25:4).

In the Old Testament social order the poor received an economic advantage. The people were commanded to loan freely to the poor, but not to charge interest (Dt. 15:7-11; Ex. 22:25). Part of the wheat and grape harvest was to be left ungathered for the benefit of the poor (Lev. 19:9-10; 23:22). Significantly, part of the purpose of the tithe was to provide relief for the poor (Dt. 14:29; 26:12-13).

The Old Testament insists that God requires justice for the poor and will judge those who oppress them. God's words by the prophet Zechariah are typical: "Render true judgments, show kindness and mercy each to his brother, do not oppress the widow, the fatherless, the sojourner, or the poor" (Zech. 7:9-10; compare Lev. 19:15; Dt. 16:18-20, 24:14-22; Prov. 31:9; Amos 2:6-7).

Finally, the Old Testament teaches that God's people bear a special ethical responsibility for the poor. Remembering their slavery in Egypt was to motivate the Israelites to show mercy to the oppressed (Dt. 24:17-22). The faithfulness of God's people was continually measured by their treatment of the poor.

All these teachings about the poor are part of God's Word. Although they are tied to specific historical contexts, the ethical message shines through and forms the background of Jesus' own attitude and teaching. The teaching is clear, consistent and persistent. Of all peoples and classes, God especially has compassion on the poor, and his acts in history confirm this.

It is relevant here to ask *why* God is thus concerned for the poor. What is there within the nature of God which prompts such special attention? To answer this fully we would have to consider in detail the biblical concept of *justice*. In the Old Testament God's concern with the poor is consistently tied to God's justice and the working of justice among God's people. Thus, biblically, words such as *the poor, the needy, the oppressed, the sojourner* typically have moral content, pointing to God's requirement for justice.

This is not easily grasped in today's world. "The poor" does not have such moral content for us. It has a merely descriptive sense; one might say that for us "poor" is a purely secular word. To be biblical, we must see that poverty itself is of ethical significance. *The poor* is a moral category. In God's world there is no human condition which escapes moral significance, and the poor, and the treatment they receive, are strong indicators of the faithfulness of God's people.

Jesus and the Poor

But what of Jesus and the poor? Did Jesus play down the Old Testament emphasis, or did he affirm it? Several facts about Jesus' attitude shine through in the Gospels.

1. *Jesus made the preaching of the gospel to the poor a validation of his own ministry.* He said, "The Spirit of the Lord is upon me, because he has anointed me to bring good news to the poor" (Lk. 4 18). He cited Isaiah 61 to show by what marks his gospel could be known. He plainly said that it was his *practice* and *conscious intent* to preach his gospel especially to the poor. (Compare Mt. 11:1-6.)

Jesus did not preach one thing and do another. His earthly ministry was of and among the poor. As G. K. Chesterton wrote, Jesus was "a stranger upon the earth" who

> *shared the drifting life of the most homeless and hopeless of the poor. . . . [H]e would quite certainly have been moved on by the police and almost certainly arrested . . . for having no visible means of subsistence. For our law has in it a turn of humor or touch of fancy which Nero and Herod never happened to think of; that of actually punishing homeless people for not sleeping at home.*[2]

2. *Jesus believed the poor were more ready and able to understand and accept his gospel.* An amazing thing, and how different from common attitudes today! One time Jesus prayed, "I thank you, Father, Lord of heaven and earth, because you have hidden these things from the wise and the intelligent, and revealed them to infants; yes, Father, for such was your gracious will" (Mt. 11:25-26). Here Jesus showed that "the wise and the intelligent"—the sophisticated, the educated, those of higher social status—find the gospel difficult

to accept, a stumbling block, while children—those of little sophistication and understanding—are quick to grasp the meaning of, and accept, the good news. Clearly the poor are in the latter category. "While he was Lord of the whole world, he preferred *children and ignorant persons to the wise*," said John Calvin.[3]

3. *Jesus specifically directed the gospel call to the poor.* He said, "Come to me, all you that are weary and carrying heavy burdens, and I will give you rest" (Mt. 11:28). Despite our ingrained tendency to spiritualize these words, it seems clear that Jesus here was speaking, in the first place, literally. Jesus' call was pre-eminently to the poor—those who, of all people, are the most wearied and burdened, not only spiritually but also from long hours of physical labor and the various oppressions known only to the poor. To these—not exclusively, but pre-eminently—Jesus speaks. Walter Rauschenbusch was right: "The fundamental sympathies of Jesus were with the poor and oppressed."[4]

4. *On several occasions Jesus recommended showing partiality to the poor.* Examine Matthew 19:21 and Luke 12:33 and 14:12-14. In this he was in complete harmony with the spirit of God's revelation in the Old Testament.

In short, Jesus Christ, the Son of God, demonstrated the same attitude toward the poor that God revealed in the Old Testament. Though the Savior of all, he looked with special compassion upon the poor. He purposely took the gospel to the poor, and specifically called attention to what he was doing.

This, in brief summary, is the biblical evidence. That there *is* biblical evidence for God's special concern for the poor is obvious if one takes the trouble to look for it.

The Gospel to the Poor Today

What do biblical teachings about the poor mean for our churches today? The implications are clear and urgent.

1. *Like her Master, the Church must place special emphasis on the poor.* A biblical theology for today must reflect the biblical concern for the poor. A church that seeks to be New Testament in spirit and practice will need to think through the implications of this key biblical emphasis.

This truth must be urgently affirmed today because contemporary Protestantism is, in general, neglecting poorer people. Bruce

Kendrick in his book on the East Harlem Protestant Parish put it this way: "Instead of seeking the lost sheep—whether black or white or speckled—[Protestants] sought out those who thought as they thought, and dressed as they dressed, and talked as they talked." Instead of seeking the poor, the church "was cutting itself off from them and neglecting the fact that the sign of the Kingdom is that the poor have the Gospel preached to them."[5] "By leaving the ghetto behind," wrote David McKenna, "the church has implied that its mission is meaningless to the poor, the hopeless, and the wretched—except when an ocean separates the church from the ghetto."[6] North American churches seem even more callous to the poor now than they were in the 1970s.

These criticisms cut uncomfortably close. Not that Protestant denominations do not have poor or working class people in them; many do. The point is the almost total lack of awareness of the church's responsibility to *seek out* the poor, to plan for church growth among them, rather than to treat the poor primarily as a social problem to be discussed and analyzed. "I was hungry, and you gave me a press release."

In America, the gospel to the poor implies a special Christian responsibility for the inner city, for the inner city is the particular kingdom of the poor. "The life of the inner city is a mixture of many things; nevertheless, its dominant note is poverty," Gibson Winter reminds us.[7]

The poor, of course, are not confined to the inner city. There are poor suburbs as well as middle-class and upper-class ones. Also, urbanization patterns vary from country to country, and the poor are not always to be found in the central city. Often they are found in the urban outer ring, as in São Paulo, Brazil. But wherever the poor are found, there is the focus of Christian responsibility.

The basic issue is not a question of geography. Christian faithfulness is not necessarily measured by where one lives, although in some cases it may be. The basic issue is Christian responsibility for the poor. If Christians move from a particular area, they must ask themselves what this move means for their responsibility toward the poor. What are their motives for moving? Where can they best build the church and incarnate God's love? Are they leaving the poor behind? If so, whose responsibility are these poor? Does the move represent greater or less obedience to the gospel? Facing such hard questions in the light of Scripture may be the only way to break the pattern of leaving the poor spiritually disinherited.

2. *The priority among the poor is evangelism*—living and telling good news. Our concern must be, in the first instance, with the central truth of the gospel message: reconciliation with God through the blood of Jesus Christ.

Jesus himself set this priority: "The Spirit of the Lord is upon me, because he has anointed me *to bring good news to the poor*" (Lk. 4:18). "The blind receive their sight, the lame walk, the lepers are cleansed, the deaf hear, the dead are raised, and the poor have *good news brought* to them" (Mt. 11:5).

In our concern for the poor, we are in critical danger of neglecting or withholding the most important thing: the message of the gospel itself. Nothing we can do for the poor is more relevant than evangelism. As Ernest Campbell wrote, "A church so busily at work correcting the massive injustices of society that it cannot or will not make the effort to win men and women to an allegiance to Jesus Christ will soon become sterile and unable to produce after its kind."[8] Nor will its kind be worth producing after.

Today many Christians are a little embarrassed, or so it seems, to talk of evangelizing the poor because of past excesses and a one-sided preoccupation with "souls." This is understandable, but no excuse for abandoning the proclamation of the good news. The gospel shared and lived must be the primary emphasis—not because it is the way to attack social problems but because "the wages of sin is death, but the free gift of God is eternal life" (Rom. 6:23). The problem of poverty may one day be solved, but the poor—or formerly poor—will still be left without the gospel.

Obviously, Christ-centered witness will not compartmentalize. It will not divide up people into "soul" and "body," caring for the one and condemning those who care for the other. "Like our Lord, who healed the sick and fed the hungry, we must see [men and women] as whole [people], not as disembodied souls to be prepackaged for heaven."[9] Thus Christ-centered evangelism will care for people—people in sin, people lost and oppressed, laboring and heavy laden people, hungry for real food and for real fellowship. It will walk as Christ walked, but it will always tell why Christ died. It will proclaim Jesus as human example, but supremely as risen Lord.

Another fact suggests the priority of evangelism: The poor are, in general, more receptive to the gospel. Jesus was right!

Ernst Troeltsch observed some eighty years ago, "The really creative, church-forming religious movements are the work of the lower strata. . . . Need upon the one hand and the absence of an all-relativizing culture of reflection on the other hand are at home only in these strata."[10] Historically this has been true: the church grows most rapidly among the poor. Sociologically speaking, the roots of Christianity have most often been among the masses. Troeltsch also wrote, "The Early Church sought and won her new adherents chiefly among the lower classes in the cities, . . . members of the well-to-do, educated upper classes only began to enter the Church in the second century, and then only very gradually."[11] Tertullian could say in the second century, "The uneducated are always a majority with us." John Wesley said in 1771, "Everywhere we find the laboring part of mankind the readiest to receive the Gospel."[12]

Church growth studies show the same pattern. One good example is the case of Adoniram Judson, famous missionary to Burma. Judson sought out the higher class Burmese as the people to evangelize. But along the way he took in a poor member of the despised and uneducated Karen tribe. This man, Ko Tha Byu, became a thorough Christian and began carrying the gospel to his own people, while Judson worked with the social elite. What happened? Great numbers of Karens turned to Christ, while relatively little fruit was seen by Judson.[13] Obviously other factors were also at work here, but a characteristic pattern appears: rapid growth of the faith among the poor.

Many similar examples come from the history of Christian missions in the last two centuries, particularly in India. Donald McGavran gives the following account in *Understanding Church Growth:*

> *In 1840 the American Baptists started a mission at Nellore on the eastern coast of India. For twenty-five years they labored among the upper castes gaining less than a hundred converts.*
>
> *In 1865 John Clough and his wife came out as new missionaries. As they learned the language and studied the Bible to see what God would have them do, each independently came to the*

conclusion that, on the basis of 1 Corinthians 1:26-28, the policy followed rigorously by the elder missionaries of seeking to win only the upper castes was displeasing to God. The Madigas (untouchables) known to be responsive to the Christian message, had been bypassed lest their baptism make it still more difficult for caste Hindus to become Christians. The Cloughs moved from Nellore, opened the station of Ongole, and began baptizing some remarkably earnest and spiritual Madiga leaders. By 1869 hundreds were being added to the Lord.[14]

In his significant study of church growth in Brazil, William R. Read noted a similar pattern, especially among Pentecostals: "People in the lower strata of Brazilian society generally accept the Christian message more readily than the more privileged who are found in the upper classes." And this is a predominantly urban pattern: "The Pentecostals have been active and successful in the highly populated urban centers to which flow large numbers of migrating peoples from rural districts."[15] I could see this in Brazil.

It is no secret that many of today's great denominations—hardly now to be classed as poor—had their beginning as Christward movements among the lower classes. The period of phenomenal growth came during those years when the gospel was preached to the poor.

This fact of rapid church growth among the poor says something about strategy and stewardship. As McGavran points out, planting the gospel seed where it is most likely to grow is faithful stewardship of the gospel message. I am convinced that Jesus commands us to preach the gospel to the poor not only because their need is most acute but also precisely because they are most ready to accept. The poor are the seedbed of spiritual and social revolution; radical renewal.

In short, both concern for personal conversion and considerations of church growth strategy say: The first priority among the poor is evangelism.

3. *Christian responsibility toward the poor does not end with evangelism.* Why? Because biblically it cannot. Because loving involvement with persons, once begun, cannot just be turned off. Parents who love their children do not neglect their needs. They feed and clothe them—not because they are unconcerned about

their souls but because in practice love is not greatly concerned with analytical distinctions between soul and body.

Therefore—since Christian responsibility toward the poor must be an expression of love—we cannot make rigid prescriptions about what exactly is Christian responsibility to the poor, beyond evangelism. Love will identify and meet the need in each specific context, if not walled in by unbiblical traditions that asphyxiate love.

We do have the Bible to guide us. It is clear from both the Old and New Testaments, for example, that God expects his people to see that the poor among them are cared for. Can we say with David, "I have not seen the righteous forsaken or his children begging bread" (Ps. 37:25)? If not, we may question whether our church is meeting its biblical responsibility to the poor.

4. *The church needs the poor.* In fact, to maintain its spiritual dynamic it needs the poor much more than it needs the rich or the middle class.

Starting with Ernst Troeltsch, students of the church as social phenomenon have observed how religious movements are born among the poor and then with succeeding generations climb the socioeconomic ladder, leaving the poor behind, disinherited. H. Richard Niebuhr's *Social Sources of Denominationalism* (published in 1929) is still very relevant at this point. Said Niebuhr, "The churches of the poor all become middle-class churches sooner or later." Niebuhr documented the following now familiar pattern:

> *One phase of the history of denominationalism reveals itself as the story of the religiously neglected poor who fashion a new type of Christianity which corresponds to their distinctive needs, who rise in the economic scale under the influence of religious discipline, and who in the midst of a freshly acquired cultural respectability, neglect the new poor succeeding them on the lower plane. This pattern recurs with remarkable regularity in the history of Christianity.*[16]

The question is, Is this pattern biblical? And is it inevitable, predestined? Clearly it is not biblical—not Christian—to neglect the poor, even though it is a common pattern. And if not biblical, neither is it inevitable. The church needs the poor. The churches of the middle class need the lower classes. If they would avoid spiritual and social hardening of the arteries, churches must be growing among the poor.

Every denomination needs a continuing infusion of hundreds of new members from among the poor—men and women saved right out of the crisis of their poverty. This would keep us shaken up and spiritually alive. It would keep our churches from being captured by any one class or political creed, and thus from being compromised. Our radical differences in the world would unite us in Christ. Fellowship in the church would demand miracle. It would be the fellowship, literally, of the Holy Spirit. Impossible? It happened in the first century A.D.

The pattern of the flesh is for our churches to grow up into "respectability," leaving the poor behind. The pattern of the Spirit is for the church to grow up into Christ, as we read in Ephesians 4.

It is not surprising that Christians do, with time, tend to prosper materially. Increased faithfulness at work, more careful stewardship of money, a new concern for education, and similar factors do bring economic and social advancement. Christian faithfulness generally brings material blessings.

The problem is not that Christians prosper; it is that in prospering they tend to turn their backs on the poor and adopt the social attitudes of their newly acquired status. Consciousness of the gospel's special call to the poor is forgotten or spiritualized.

According to the Bible, the pattern should be different. In prospering materially, Christians should make special effort to spread the gospel among the poor. They now have the material resources to do this! Pastors and Christian leaders should continually point to this biblical responsibility and help Christians fulfill it. This is necessary not only for the sake of the poor but also for the spiritual health of those who are not poor.

The church needs the poor. As her members naturally prosper materially "under the influence of religious discipline"—a legitimate fruit, if not a guaranteed result, of the gospel—she must deliberately, self-consciously, preach the gospel to the poor. The church needs constantly the spiritual dynamism, spontaneity, honesty and radical dedication found pre-eminently among the poor who have heeded the call of Christ. The way to radical renewal and consistent growth may lie precisely here: in effective ministry among the masses. A healthy emphasis on the gospel to the poor may be the surest antidote to institutionalism and brittle wineskins.

The Practice of the Principles

What does all this mean in practice? How can churches today be faithful to the poor?

The first step is *awareness* of this responsibility—still largely lacking—and *commitment* to do something about it. What I have said here is intended as a step in that direction.

Beyond this, we should seek a biblical approach. This means that we do not automatically assume the necessity of elaborate building- or organization-centered programs. The approach should be people-centered through personal witness, informal contacts, person-to-person (rather than primarily mass) communication and small Bible study groups in homes or other places. The first priority should be to form a nucleus of solid disciples, then to use this primary cell to move out both in evangelism and social ministry to reach the larger community. Often the poor themselves, once solidly converted, can do more for Christ in their own communities than can imported, highly trained and well-funded specialists, primarily because they see the problems from the inside and feel their weight. They live them.[17]

The need, therefore, is not for expensive, large-scale programs to carry the gospel to the poor—a fundamental but wrong and essentially worldly assumption that people make when witness among the poor is considered. The need is for ordinary committed Christians with the vision and dedication to work among the poor, to spend time with them, to live among them in some cases, to form, quietly and without fanfare, dynamic cells of Christian witness which multiply to transform the community for Christ.[18]

Such an approach automatically answers most questions about finances. Ministry among the poor is not expensive if based on biblical principles. Nothing can be clearer from the New Testament itself and from early church history. The initial "missionaries" may be supported by a local church or group of Christian families, or they may be self-supporting. But once a nucleus of converts has been formed, its own tithe will be sufficient to carry on the work. The expense is not monetary. It is, rather, the cost of discipleship.

This is not, of course, to rule out entirely the possibility of major church-sponsored programs of relief or social action among the poor. These can be helpful. But they are really secondary forms of Christian ministry; no substitute for evangelism among the poor on a more personal basis.

But is the ideal possible, given the contemporary situation? Can a middle-class church (for example) convincingly preach the gospel to the poor? If not, the ever-new wine of the gospel will burst the old wineskins and once again create new ones. Rich churches will be left to die, becoming Laodicean (Rev. 3:17), and the true church will once again spring up among the poor. This is happening now in some places, as it has repeatedly in history.

In Brazil, China, and elsewhere the poor are responding to the good news. But in my mind's ear I hear someone "back home" objecting, "Yes, but that's on the mission field!" Indeed it is— places like São Paulo, Brazil, a sophisticated and growing city of fifteen million people. But today the whole world is a mission field—a mission field of cities. The urban poor have the same needs and the same hunger for Christ whether in São Paulo, Manila, or Chicago. We think that in our land the response would not be the same if the gospel were preached to the poor. But then, how do we know? We aren't there. We haven't tried.

There must be a new preaching of the gospel to the poor in our day. The biblical gospel demands it. What we should hope and pray for, what we should expect, is not merely a host of individual churches that are growing and dynamic. Our hope should be to touch off revolutionary spiritual movements that "get out of (our) control," but are led by the Holy Spirit. It has happened before. It is happening right now in some places. It can happen again.

We must have nothing short of revolution—a spiritual revolution of global proportions, as occurred nineteen centuries ago. Both the Bible and church history point the same way: Preach the gospel to the poor.

But, again, *can* the gospel be preached to the poor today? Are contemporary churches in a condition to make such proclamation and live out such a gospel? The fact is that the greater part of contemporary Protestantism is caught in a stifling web of institutionalism. The wineskins have grown rigid. It is not enough, therefore, merely to call for change or to proclaim the need for proclamation. The whole problem of wineskins—the structure of the church—must be faced.

The Poor and the Problem of Wineskins

So the urgency to preach the gospel to the poor brings us right to the question of the church and the problem of wineskins. The gospel to the poor and the concept of the church are inseparably linked. Failure to minister to the poor testifies to more than unfulfilled responsibility; it witnesses to *a distorted view of the church* and the need for radical renewal.

Church history illustrates this. As I have already commented, renewal in the church has usually meant the church's rebirth among the poor, the masses, the alienated. And with such resurgence has usually come the recovery of such essential New Testament emphases as community, purity, discipleship, the priesthood of believers and the gifts of the Spirit.

The Protestant Reformation is the most striking case in point. As Niebuhr notes, "The failure of the Reformation to meet the religious needs of peasants and other disfranchised groups is a chapter writ large in history. With all its native religious fervor it remained the religion of the middle class and the nobility."[19] The Reformation trumpet call of salvation by faith wakened the hope of deliverance among the oppressed masses, but the second blast called forth the troops against those who were prepared to take the gospel call of "liberty to the oppressed" too literally. Tragically, the poor were betrayed by much of the Reformation.

Why? Doubtless the reasons are complex, involving many social, political and economic, as well as theological, factors. The significant thing for our discussion here is that the mainline Reformation focused mainly on the question of personal salvation (soteriology). It hardly touched, in any practical way, the doctrine of the church (ecclesiology), although it brought a number of structural modifications. As Hendrick Hart wrote, "Even though the leaders of the Protestant Reformation sincerely intended to break with the traditional Roman Catholic conception of the church, nevertheless the tradition arising from the Reformation did not succeed in making that break."[20]

The presbyterian and congregational systems arising from

the Reformation brought some practical improvements. But both systems rested on many an untested medieval assumption about the nature of the church. This is evident particularly in the doctrine of spiritual gifts and the general concept of ministry, where the traditional clergy-laity dichotomy was largely carried over.[21] The result is that modern Protestant churches—whether presbyterian, congregational or episcopal in form—are more impressive for their similarity than for their differences. Regardless of the label, most Protestant ecclesiology is based more on tradition than on Scripture.

The result of the mainline Reformation's neglect of the poor and of the doctrine of the church was the so-called Radical Reformation, and principally the Anabaptist Movement. According to Roland Bainton, Anabaptism was "the result of an effort to carry through more consistently the program of the restoration of primitive Christianity. . . . Much more drastically than any of their contemporaries [the Anabaptists] searched the Scriptures in order to recover the pattern of the early church."[22]

Anabaptism, as well as such related movements as Quakerism, "the Anglo-Saxon parallel to Anabaptism"[23] a century later, was largely a movement of the peasants and the poorer classes. In their radical simplicity, these groups sought to carry through the Reformation impulse to the practical level of the daily life and witness of the Christian community. Theologically, this was an extension of the Reformation to ecclesiology and church structure.

The result for the Anabaptists, of course, was persecution or extermination. The best Anabaptist leaders were soon eliminated "by fire, water, and sword," often at the hands of the mainline Reformers or their followers.[24] But a remnant survived. Later such groups as the Mennonites and the Hutterites, through much suffering and persecution, carried on the same ideals.

It is beside the point that some among the Anabaptists, Mennonites, Quakers and similar groups, under pressure of persecution, occasionally went to extremes. The significant thing is that these movements of "the gospel to the poor" sought to restore a more biblical understanding and practice of the church. Church history since the Reformation shows that it is precisely these groups (or the re-evaluation of them) that have sparked much of the contemporary impulse to re-examine the doctrine and structure of the church.

The need today is certainly not to attempt to mimic the radical reformers or to try now to carry through their program of reform.[25] The need is rather to see the importance of the New Testament understanding of the church for our day, to insist that "salvation by faith" must be connected to true Christian community and real discipleship. In the Reformation age that idea was too radical to be tolerated. Today it is not. Today when new things are happening and fresh winds are blowing, the problem of wineskins needs examination by those who would take seriously Jesus Christ's announcement that he came to preach the gospel to the poor.

It is to this problem that we now turn our attention, first looking critically at some old wineskins and then suggesting the way to some fresh ones.

A Look At Old Wineskins

Churches, Temples and Tabernacles

LET'S GO BACK to the Old Testament for a moment.

We can learn a lot from Moses. The Mosaic covenant and the forty years in the wilderness not only formed the Hebrew faith; they also teach us much about the nature of the community of God's people—about the church.

The three central elements in the Mosaic covenant were *sacrifice, priesthood* and *tabernacle*. These together, as part of and coupled with the Mosaic law, constituted the revealed basis for the covenant relationship between God and his chosen people. They established the approved way to God, *atonement,* God dwelling with his people in covenant fidelity.

The amazing teaching of the New Testament, especially in the book of Hebrews, is that Jesus Christ is the fulfillment of *sacrifice, priesthood* and *tabernacle.* Jesus Christ is our great High Priest; therefore we need no earthly priest (Heb. 4:14; 8:1). The priesthood has passed away—or rather has been expanded to include all believers (1 Pet. 2:9; Rev. 1:6).

So also Jesus Christ is the true and perfect sacrifice, offered once for all. No other sacrifice is either necessary or possible (Heb. 7:27; 9:14, 25-28; 1 Pet. 3:18). The sacrificial system has become completely superfluous because all that was prefigured in the Mosaic covenant was fulfilled in the death of Christ. There is no more sacrifice, except as the church presents herself as a "living sacrifice" (Rom. 12:1-2) and offers "the sacrifice of praise" (Heb. 13:15).

It is also true, but much less emphasized, that Jesus Christ is the fulfillment of the tabernacle (Heb. 8-9). "For Christ did not enter a sanctuary made by human hands, a mere copy of the true one, but he entered into heaven itself, now to appear in the presence of God on our behalf" (Heb. 9:24). Thus the need for an earthly tabernacle has passed away. "The Word became flesh and lived [literally, tabernacled] among us" (Jn. 1:14; compare Jn. 1:17). Jesus identified his body with the temple (Jn. 2:19-21).[1] He is Emmanuel, "God with us" (Mt. 1:23).

Christ's body is, in one sense, "the true tabernacle." Thus the community of believers, the "body of Christ," is also part of the true tabernacle. For the church is "God's house" (Heb. 3:6; I Tim. 3:15), a "holy temple" (Eph. 2:21; 2 Cor. 6:16), a "dwelling place for God" (Eph. 2:22).

Sacrifice, priesthood, tabernacle—all instituted through Moses in the Old Testament. Theologically, all passed away with the coming of Christ and the birth of the church. Historically, all passed away with the destruction of Jerusalem in 70 A.D. They had become irrelevant, anachronistic. Old wineskins.

And so the church was born without priesthood, sacrifice or tabernacle because the church and Christ together were all three. The church faithfully embodied this truth for more than a century, and overran the Roman Empire.

The great temptation of the organized church has been to reinstate these three elements among God's people: to turn community into an institution. Historically, the church has at times succumbed. Returning to the spirit of the Old Testament, she has set up a professional priesthood, turned the Eucharist into a new sacrificial system and built great cathedrals. When this happens, a return to faithfulness must mean a return—in both soteriology and ecclesiology—to the profound simplicity of the New Testament. Usually, however, reformation in doctrine has not been tied to sufficiently radical reform in church structure.

The Importance of the Tabernacle

The significance of the tabernacle must be singled out for special attention here—partly because it usually is not, but primarily because it has significance for the church, for ecclesiology. Why should God be represented by a physical structure? Why a tent?

In the Mosaic covenant the tabernacle was the symbol of God's presence. "Have them make me a sanctuary, that I may dwell among them" (Ex. 25:8). The central idea was God's *habitation*

56

with his people. God could not actually dwell in the hearts of the people because of their sin and rebelliousness; his habitation had to be symbolic. So God ordered up the tabernacle, laying it out to Moses in extravagant detail. It was to be built according to the blueprint revealed on the mount (Ex. 26:30; Acts 7:44; Heb. 8:5).

But for the church the tabernacle is fulfilled in the body of Christ, as we have seen. So the necessity of a physical tabernacle has passed away. Why? Because now God dwells with his people in the hearts and bodies of the believing community, through the inhabiting of the Holy Spirit. The Holy Spirit "abides with you, and will be in you" (Jn. 14:17), Jesus said. If any love and obey Jesus, the Father and Son "will come to them and make our home with them" (Jn. 14:23). "I will come in and eat with you, and you with me" (Rev. 3:20).

Clearly, the central idea of the tabernacle is God's habitation. But in the New Testament God dwells within the hearts of his people, not just symbolically among them. The veil has been torn in two; the stony heart transplanted with one of flesh. So the church is "a dwelling place of God" in and through the Spirit (Eph. 2:22).

There will also be an eternal, eschatological fulfillment of the idea of God's habitation. When John sees the holy city descending from God, the first words he hears from the throne are, "Behold, the tabernacle of God is with" men and women (Rev. 21:3, AV; compare Ezek. 37:27-28). This is the meaning of the holy city: God's habitation eternally, spiritually, really and perfectly, with his people. Therefore naturally there is "no temple in the city, for its temple is the Lord God the Almighty and the Lamb" (Rev. 21:22). And has this not ever been God's design: a city without temples because God himself is its temple? Here all limitations of time and space have evaporated. God and his people in perfect communion. Eternally, God's people dwelling in the fellowship, the *koinonia*, of the Holy Spirit.

So we see a threefold progression: First, God symbolically dwelling *among* his people in a physical structure called a tabernacle. Second, God actually dwelling *within the hearts and in the community* of his people through the Holy Spirit. Third, God dwelling *eternally* with his people, *in perfect unbroken communion*, in the age to come. The first reality points to the second, and the second to the third.

Tabernacle or Temple?

But in going from Moses to Christ, we jump over 1200 years

of the history of God's people—the age of the temple. With the reign of David and Solomon the tabernacle was replaced by the temple. Are tabernacle and temple identical in meaning? Or do they suggest different aspects of God's plan?

Analyzing the Old Testament account, we can see a distinct difference between tabernacle and temple.

I marvel every time I read of the construction of the ark and the tabernacle in the Old Testament. This was the pattern of the Ark of the Covenant:

> *Make an ark of acacia wood, two cubits and a half shall be its length, a cubit and a half its breadth, and a cubit and a half its height. And you shall overlay it with pure gold, . . . And you shall cast four rings of gold for it and put them on its four feet, . . . And you shall put the poles into the rings on the sides of the ark to carry the ark by them (Ex. 25:11-14).*

On top of this chest went the mercy seat, a magnificent golden cover with two cherubim, their wings stretched over the ark.

Consider this beautiful and costly creation, symbol of the presence of Almighty God, Creator of the universe—but with two poles sticking out the ends for carrying it! A marred symbol? No, a perfect symbol—symbol not only of a holy God, but also of a mobile God! God has not been captured there in the tent. Some day, maybe tomorrow, things are going to change. The cloud will start to move. The ark will be carried on. Yahweh is free to be unpredictable. He is always true to himself, but not necessarily to our preconceptions. He will do a new thing.

The tabernacle is the symbol of God's presence with his people, and as such it is, supremely, a mobile symbol. Everything is made to be easily dismounted and carried. And this is not Moses' idea; it is according to the pattern revealed on the mountain, as Scripture says repeatedly. If the tabernacle represents God's presence, it certainly represents the dynamic nature of God and the mobility of God's people.

But, it may be objected, this is pressing the meaning too far. Naturally the tabernacle had to be movable, for God's people were on a journey. Its mobility has no further significance. But this is precisely the point! *God* initiated the journey; *he* required it to last forty years; *he* created a pilgrim people. This was Israel's great object lesson about the nature of their God. Before settling down in the promised land, they must learn what kind of God they serve. He is not a God to be confined to a land or a city or a temple; he is beyond all these. The only way to truly learn this is as a pilgrim people, and the tabernacle reflects this.

One of the most beautiful and radical passages in the Old Testament graphically pictures this mobility:

> *Whenever the cloud lifted from the tent, the Israelites struck camp, and at the place where the cloud settled, there they pitched their camp. At the command of the LORD they struck camp, and at the command of the LORD they encamped again, and contin- ued in camp as long as the cloud rested over the Tabernacle. When the cloud stayed long over the Tabernacle, the Israelites remained in attendance on the LORD and did not move on; and it was the same when the cloud continued over the Tabernacle only a few days: at the command of the LORD they remained in camp; and at the command of the LORD they struck camp. There were also times when the cloud continued only from evening till morning, and in the morning, when the cloud lifted, they moved on. Whether by day or by night, they moved as soon as the cloud lifted. Whether it was for a day or two, for a month or a year, whenever the cloud stayed long over the Tabernacle, the Israelites remained where they were and did not move on; they did so only when the cloud lifted. At the command of the LORD they encamped, and at his command they struck camp. At the LORD's command given through Moses, they remained in attendance on the LORD (Num. 9:17-23, NEB).*

So it was with the tabernacle. But the temple was different. It was stationary—anchored, permanent—and its meaning differs accordingly.

The tabernacle was God's idea; it was his design. He command- ed it. But what of the temple? God sent word to King David,

> *Are you the one to build me a house to live in? I have not lived in a house since the day I brought up the people of Israel from Egypt to this day, but I have been moving about in a tent and a*

tabernacle. Wherever I have moved about among all the people of Israel, did I speak a word with any of the tribal leaders of Israel, whom I commanded to shepherd my people Israel, saying, "Why have you not built me a house of cedar?" (2 Sam. 7:5-7).

King David was rich, prosperous and at peace. He said to Nathan the prophet, "See now, I am living in a house of cedar, but the ark of God stays in a tent" (2 Sam. 7:2). If the king has a royal house, why not God, too? Is it not logical? The recognition of proper priorities?

Thus the temple was David's idea, not God's. Further, David was king, and the monarchy was not God's idea either (1 Sam. 8:4-9). We may wonder whether there would ever have been a temple had there not been a king. But in both cases God accommodated his plan to human desires, for his own purposes.

God allowed the temple to be built, but not by David. David made preparations but Solomon did the building. In contrast to the tabernacle, the blueprint did not come from Mount Sinai. God was not the architect.

While Solomon was building the temple, a word came from God: "Concerning this house which you [note, *you*, not *I*] are building, if you will walk in my statutes, obey my ordinances, and keep all my commandments by walking in them, then I will establish my promise with you, which I made to your father David. I will dwell among the children of Israel, and will not forsake my people Israel" (1 Kings. 6:12-13). Although the temple is not God's idea, he honors Solomon's good intentions, even his creativity. God will dwell in the house; he will continue the covenant—*provided* Solomon and the people are faithful.[2]

Such was the beginning of the temple. Later the people disobeyed God and the temple was destroyed. The chosen people were carried away prisoner. They thought God was safely within the temple and among the priests, but suddenly he came at them from outside, through the voice of the prophet and the thunder of foreign kings.

The conclusion from all this is clear: The truer sign of the presence of God in his earthly church is the tabernacle, and only secondarily the temple. The tabernacle is the truer symbol, for it more accurately shows how God acts in history.

A certain legitimacy does belong to the Old Testament temple, but this is essentially typological and eschatological, based on the Davidic kingdom as the type of Christ's eternal kingdom.[3] The typology comes through clearly in the Psalms, where David is the king, Jerusalem is the holy city and the temple is God's holy dwelling. But the primary significance is eschatological. In actual fact David sins, the monarchy degenerates, the holy city is full of blood and the temple worship finally falls into a dead institutionalism.

This typical, eschatological interpretation is borne out further by what the prophets say about the temple. They frequently speak of a temple, but usually it is God's eternal temple in heaven to which they refer.[4] Ezekiel's vision of the temple certainly has eschatological significance, as is clear from parallels with the book of Revelation. Further, Jeremiah warns against a false faith in the temple: "Do not trust in these deceptive words, 'This is the temple of the LORD, the temple of the LORD, the temple of the LORD'" (Jer. 7:4).

An apparent exception to this view of the temple is found in the postexilic rebuilding of the temple, and particularly in Haggai's prophecy. Here—for the only time in the Bible—God commands a temple to be built (Hag. 1:7-8).

Haggai had four visions within a span of four months. The temple lay in ruins, but the people were more preoccupied with embellishing their own homes than with rebuilding God's house. In the first vision God commands them to rebuild the temple. Why? Because the people had left their first love. The temple had become the symbol of God's presence, and their neglect of it was sign and symptom of their neglect of God himself.

But in the succeeding visions, also relating to the temple, God's will is put into eschatological perspective. God says, in effect, "Do you see how this temple you are rebuilding is only a shadow of the glory of the former? But the time is coming when things will change." God says, "I will fill this house with glory; . . . and the glory of this latter house shall surpass the glory of the former" (Hag. 2:3-9, NEB). The reference here is to the eschatological future (as in other similar passages) and not to the immediate future of the physical temple, which could not (and never did) compare with the earlier, Solomonic temple.

What is the point of Haggai's prophecy, then? Simply that the people were being unfaithful to God, and God commanded the rebuilding of the temple as an act of rededication to the covenant made with Solomon.

But even here the earthly temple is not permitted to assume undue importance. Immediately it is put into eternal perspective: The physical temple is only the shadow of what is to come in God's future kingdom, when God shakes heaven and earth, sea and land (Hag. 2:21-23).

Even Isaiah's sublime vision in Isaiah 6 lends no legitimacy to the earthly temple. His eyes were opened to see God on his eternal throne, in his heavenly temple. The imagery is clearly that of the celestial temple, not of the earthly one. (Compare Rev. 4:1-11). Interestingly, the passage does not even say Isaiah was in the temple when the vision came, although we usually assume this. He may have been resting in his own house.

We see, then, in the tabernacle and the desert wandering the Old Testament counterpart of the church in history as God's pilgrim people. The temple and the kingdom more truly represent Christ's eschatological kingdom, to be fulfilled in the age to come. Both the tabernacle and the temple represent God's habitation with his people. But the simpler, unpretentious, wandering tabernacle is the truer symbol of the church on earth.[5]

Tabernacle and Church

With the birth of the church the need for a physical tabernacle or temple passed away. No longer was a temple needed. There was no longer any one holy place for worship and sacrifice (Jn. 4:20-24), for the sacrifice had already been made, once and for all. All that was necessary was a place to meet together as the Christian community. The most natural place was the home (Acts 2:46; 5:42). Jewish Christians continued worshipping for some time in the temple, but the practice tapered off. And the temple was destroyed in 70 A.D.

It is striking that Stephen in his appeal in the temple prior to his martyrdom goes directly from a discussion of the tabernacle and the temple to his condemnation of the Jewish leaders:

> *Our ancestors had the tent of testimony in the wilderness, as God directed when he spoke to Moses, ordering him to make it according to the pattern that he had seen. . . And it was there*

until the days of David, who found favor with God and asked that he might find a dwelling place for the house of Jacob. But it was Solomon who built a house for him. Yet the Most High does not dwell in houses made with human hands (Acts 7:44-48).

The point here seems to be the Jewish leaders' slowness of heart to recognize the true signs of God's presence. They "resist the Holy Spirit" by trusting in the physical temple, failing to see Jesus Christ as the fulfillment of both tabernacle and temple, as both priest and king. So accustomed to looking for God in stone and mortar, they do not recognize him in human flesh (Jn. 1:1-11). They have rejected Jesus Christ and are trusting in that which no more has meaning.

All of this suggests a most basic fact: *Theologically, the church does not need temples.* Church buildings are not essential to the true nature of the church. For the meaning of the tabernacle is God's habitation, and God already dwells within the human community of Christian believers. *The people* are the temple and the tabernacle, a tabernacle "not made with hands," a "greater and more perfect tent" of which the Mosaic tabernacle was but a copy (Heb. 9:11). Thus, theologically, church buildings are superfluous. They are not needed for priestly functions because all believers are priests and all have direct access, at whatever time and place, to the one great High Priest. A church building cannot properly be "the Lord's house" because in the new covenant this title is reserved for the church *as people* (Eph. 2; 1 Tim. 3:15; Heb. 10:21). A church building cannot be a "holy place" in any special sense, for holy places no longer exist, and all creation is sacred. Christianity has no holy *places,* only holy *people.* Christians know that God is present everywhere, for the earth is the Lord's.

It is hard to find biblical support for constructing church buildings. On the contrary, the teaching of Hebrews—which most clearly asserts that the sacrificial system and the priesthood have passed away so that the church now needs neither—may imply that the church should not become involved in building churches any more than it should institute a new priesthood or a new sacrifice.[6] In any case, the early church did not build church buildings.[7]

The conclusion that the church, theologically, does not need buildings is reinforced by the distinction we have seen between tabernacle and temple. We have noted God's apparent preference for the tabernacle over the temple as the sign of his habitation with his people, for the tabernacle emphasizes God as dynamic not static; as mobile, as a God of surprises. And it thus shows God's people—the church—as mobile and flexible, as pilgrims. But the image of the temple is strikingly incompatible with the idea of a pilgrim people. There is a certain incongruity to the portable Ark of the Covenant resting securely within Solomon's temple. A temple cannot be moved; it can only be destroyed. It is static. And so in the Bible God does not command the church to build temples. The tabernacle is the truer sign of his presence, and even it has been fulfilled and has passed away.

So if church buildings have any justification, it can only be practical—simply a place to meet and carry on essential functions, as necessary. Beyond this, buildings become a return to the shadow of the Old Testament and a betrayal of the reality of the New.

Theologically, church building are at best unnecessary and at worst idolatrous. If the priesthood and the sacrificial system have passed away, so should the tabernacle. All three have ceased to be institutions and have become something alive, through the life-giving Spirit of Christ and through his Body, which we are.

Much of this is well said in the following words, quoted by John Havlik in *People-Centered Evangelism:*

> *"The church is never a place, but always a people; never a fold but always a flock; never a sacred building but always a believing assembly. The church is you who pray, not where you pray. A structure of brick or marble can no more be a church than your clothes of serge or satin can be you."*[8]

The church is the community of God's people, the habitation of God's Spirit.

This is the true nature of the church. And this is what the early church experienced.

Are Church Buildings Superfluous?

IN A SMALL mountain village the wind would blow gently, especially in the spring time.

High on a hill behind the village, the wind was much stronger. The people would climb there occasionally to feel the full force of the wind. The wind would sweep down from the mountains, mussing their hair, cooling their faces, taking their breath away.

In time, the villagers built a little shrine on the hilltop. They put up four walls and a roof, but left wide open windows so people could still feel the wind.

Over time they built the shrine larger and finer. But some grew concerned about the rain. Occasionally the rain would come, and would blow in through the windows. The water was leaving stains on the walls and floors and seats.

That's why they put glass in the windows. Plain, clear glass, so they could still see out, see the mountains and the valley. They would come and enjoy themselves and watch through the windows as the wind moved the trees and swept the hillside. They could no longer feel the wind, but they liked the view.

But things happen over time. Eventually the villagers, growing more prosperous, decided to decorate the windows with paintings and pictures. Finally fine stained-glass panes replaced the earlier clear glass.

The shrine still remains. It is a beautiful place—well preserved and attended. People make pilgrimages there. They enter the shrine, turn on the lights, bow in prayer, and remember what it used to feel like when the wind blew down from the mountains, mussing their hair, cooling their faces, and taking their breath away.

The Witness of Church Buildings

Just think of it!

"If you had asked, 'Where is the church?' in any important city of the ancient world where Christianity had penetrated in the first century, you would have been directed to a group of worshipping people gathered in a house. There was no special building or other tangible wealth with which to associate 'church,' only people." So wrote the late Walter Oetting in a significant little book, *The Church of the Catacombs*.[1]

Christians did not begin to build church buildings until about 200 A.D. This fact suggests that, whatever else church buildings are good for, they are not essential either for numerical growth or spiritual depth. The early church possessed both these qualities, and the church's greatest period of vitality and growth until recent times was during the first two centuries A.D. In other words, the church grew fastest when it did not have the help—or hindrance—of church buildings.

But if it is really true that church buildings are not essential either for growth or vitality, why are churches today so indebted (literally and figuratively) to them? Does the church really suffer an "edifice complex"?

Church buildings are a kind of witness. They tell five things about the church today.

First, church buildings are *a witness to our immobility*. What is more immovable than a church building? An entrenched bureaucracy, perhaps, but very little else. And yet Christians are, supposedly, wayfaring pilgrims. Christians are to be a mobile people. In the Old Testament the portable tabernacle was the symbol of God's presence in community with his people, as we noted in the previous chapter. The Old Testament did not find its fulfillment in impressive church buildings but in the fleshly temple, ordinary people.

The gospel says, "Go," but our church buildings say, "Stay." The gospel says, "Seek the lost," but our temples say, "Let the lost seek the church."

Second, church buildings are *a witness to our inflexibility*. As soon as we erect a building, we cut down on our options by at least seventy-five percent. Once the building is up and in use, the church program and budget are largely determined. The Sunday morning service allows the direct participation of only a few—dictated by the sanctuary layout. Basically the services will be a matter of one person speaking to all the rest, and this one person will be set apart and recognized as a professional—dictated by the platform arrangement. Communication will be one-way (if that is communication)—preacher to people—dictated by architecture and the PA system. And so on. Architecture petrifies program.

The problem, at heart, is not one of poor planning. It is a matter of the inherent limitations of church buildings. Buildings are, by nature, inflexible and encourage inflexibility—or worse, stagnation.[2] After a number of years as an urban minister in Los Angeles, Lawrence Carter said it this way: "At present, city churches are slaves to their brick and mortar at a time when the Church needs to be flexible, adaptable, and relevant to the very real needs, sorrows, and aspirations of a rapidly changing urban population."[3] The same could be said of the majority of suburban and small-town churches.

Third, church buildings are *a witness to our lack of fellowship.* Church building may be worshipful places, but usually they are not friendly places. They are uncomfortable and impersonal. Church buildings are not made for fellowship, for *koinonia* in the biblical sense. Homes are. And it was in homes that early Christians met for worship (Acts 2:42; 5:42). Church buildings are made for worship, but worship without fellowship becomes something cold and divorced from reality.

In probably ninety percent of all church buildings the sanctuary seating consists of wooden pews set in rows and screwed securely to the floor. The pews are arranged to make it nearly impossible for a worshipper to look into the face of any other worshipper. It is as though the ideal would be to put each worshipper in his or her own isolation booth so he or she would see only the "minister" and not be distracted by other people. But if we are to worship the Lord *together,* we need to be *together.* To communicate with each other as we worship, we must be able to see each other. We must be able to see the attentive face, the tearful eye, the quiet smile that tell us something is happening and let us enter into worship *together.*

Many congregations have sensed this lack of fellowship in the church and so have added something called a "fellowship hall." But how frequently do we attain, either in the fellowship hall, the sanctuary or the Sunday school class, anything that truly can be called fellowship? True *koinonia,* real biblical Christian fellowship such as experienced by the early Christians, is lacking in most churches today.[4]

And so a stranger may attend a Christian church for weeks and never encounter the winsome, warm, loving fellowship that draws a person to Christ. Such a situation would simply have been impossible in A.D. 100.

Fourth, church buildings are *a witness to our pride.* We insist that our church structures must be beautiful and well appointed— which usually means expensive—and justify this on the grounds that God deserves the best. But such thinking may be little more than the rationalizing of carnal pride.

Or we say, perhaps, that after all we are ambassadors for the King of kings, who is abundantly rich. True. But this does not justify spending vast resources to build embassies. We may forget that our king chooses to be a servant, and we are called to serve him by serving others.

We have other excuses for our expensive temples. We may, for instance, feel that we must have beautiful buildings in order to draw sinners to the church and thus to Christ. But two things are wrong here. First, the concept is wrong. The church is to seek the lost, not vice versa. Second, the motivation is wrong. We try to attract sinners by appealing to pride ("We certainly are pleased and honored to have Mrs. Hackett, little Sandra's mother, visiting our Sunday school today, and we hope both she and Mr. Hackett will come back next Sunday . . ."). This was not Christ's approach. Too often our churches end up competing with each other on the architectural plane. This is evangelism at its worst.

We often say that our church buildings must be in harmony, in style and value, with the architecture of the community. But this is simply a brand of conformity to the world. A gospel with New Testament dynamic does not need to make a good impression through the appeal of an attractive building. That is rather like wrapping a diamond in tinsel to help it sell. In fact, a fine church building may simply attract the Pharisees and repel the poor. That has, after all, happened before in church history. We have reworked Jesus' parable: "A certain farmer went forth to sow. But first he built a fancy barn to impress the neighbors. . . ."

Since when is it the church's task to impress people with its architecture, or to melt chameleon-like into the surrounding environment? The church is to stand for Christ *against* the vanities of human culture. This should be true even in architecture. If buildings are to be built, let them speak of God, not middle-class materialism.

Finally, church buildings are *a witness to our divisions of class and race*. The early church was a mix of rich and poor, Jew and Greek, black and white, ignorant and educated. But our church buildings are public advertisements that this is not true today. A sociologist can take a casual look at ten church buildings and their denominational brand names and then predict with high accuracy the education, income, occupations and social position of the majority of their respective members. In the light of the New Testament, this ought not to be.

But in a less sophisticated way, the new family in the community does the same thing as the sociologist. They go for a drive and look over the neighborhood church buildings. They choose one that looks like "their kind"—one that will contain people of approximately the same income, education, politics and color as themselves. In most cases, a careful look at the building and parking lot is enough to tell them whether they will "feel at home" there. Of course, occasionally they may be fooled by a lower-class church that is moving up in the world and has just completed a building program.

The fault here, of course, lies much deeper than mere architecture. But the building is a witness. It is a signpost telling the world of the church's class consciousness and exclusiveness.

Our church buildings, then, witness to the *immobility, inflexibility, lack of fellowship, pride* and *class divisions* in today's church.

What Should Be Done?

What then should be done? Should we stop using church buildings?

For many churches, this would be the best solution. A different kind of architecture is not enough. Remember, during its most vital 150 years the Christian church never even heard of church buildings. It thought "church" meant people, the community of disciples. In those days the church was mobile, flexible, friendly, humble, inclusive—and growing like mad!

We could recommend less radical solutions—less building-centered programs, more outreach, simpler architecture. But why? Why continue building temples? Why not simply do away with them? Traditional church buildings are unnecessary in an urban world and are often a hindrance to biblical Christianity.

Of course, to suggest that church buildings are needless luxuries immediately raises storms of protest:

"What would be done with all that property?" Christ's words suggest a possible response for a church with "great possessions": "Go, sell what you possess and give to the poor, . . . and come, follow me" (Mt. 19:21).

"But where would Christians meet?" In homes, as did the early Christians.[5] We would go back to "the church in your house" (Philem. 2).

"But houses are too small!" Only if the church is too big. Divide the congregation into groups of twelve to thirty people. This would facilitate fellowship and allow the members to get acquainted with each other. It could be a refreshing experience!

"But we need large-group corporate worship." True—as I argue in chapter 8. But it is sufficient for the congregation to rent a small hall or school or community center where it can meet for corporate worship and training once or twice a week, and not spend hundreds of thousands of dollars to provide a large sanctuary that is used only a few hours weekly.[6]

"But people would not be attracted to a school or storefront." Well, there are two kinds of people—those who are committed to Christ and those who are not. Those really committed to Christ and his church will meet anywhere. Those who are not, it is true, probably would not flock to a humble storefront. But this is immaterial if the church is a missionary community and if the basic unit is the small group. In this case, evangelism happens outside of "church." Hence there is no concern or reason to attract the uncommitted to the place of worship. Once they have met Christ, they will come.

6

Must Pastors Be Superstars?

MEET PASTOR JONES, Superstar.

He can preach, counsel, evangelize, administrate, conciliate, communicate and sometimes even integrate. He can also raise the budget.

He handles Sunday morning better than any talk-show host on weekday TV. He is better with words than most political candidates. As a scholar he surpasses many seminary professors. No church social function would be complete without him.

His church, of course, Counts Itself Fortunate. Alas, not many churches can boast such talent.

I confess my admiration, perhaps slightly tinged with envy. Not because of the talent, really, the sheer ability. But for the success, the accomplishment. Here is a man who faithfully preaches the Word, sees lives transformed by Christ, sees his church growing. What sincere Protestant minister would not like to be in his shoes? Not to mention his parsonage.

I think of all the struggling, mediocre pastors, looking on with holy envy (if there be such), measuring their own performance by Pastor Jones' success and dropping another notch into discouragement or, perhaps, self-condemnation.

For after all, the problem is plain, isn't it? The church needs more qualified pastors, better training. More alertness to guiding those talented young people God may be calling into "the ministry." Better talent scouting to find the superstars.

But—what if? What if the problem is not really the lack of superstars? What if something is deeply wrong with the traditional concept of ministry in the church?

Is the problem really a lack of ecclesiastical superstars? Or do we have unbiblical notions of what the church really is?

Can it be that our structures quench the Spirit?

Take Pastor Jones' church. There is Bill S——, who has unusual speaking ability. Won a debate championship in high school. He would be capable of preaching—but nobody ever thought of that. He's an usher.

Then there is John M——. Nice guy. Everyone's friend. People naturally go to him with their problems. He has a knack for listening; he even listens with his eyes. With a little training and encouragement he could have a real ministry of the healing of persons. He would also need a little more time: He's on three church committees.

Or Sherrie R——, social worker. She's effective as a Sunday school teacher, but she hurts deeply for the suffering of the poor. She's burnt out, because she's constantly giving and never receiving nurture. She's deeply talented, but really too busy to grow. Her secret dream is to see the church start a ministry of social reform, but she's too tired out.

Or Bob B——, accountant. Naturally, he is church finance chairman, and he does a fine job. No one knows he is also something of a self-taught Bible scholar—a seemingly superfluous talent.

In fact, looking into the lives of the several hundred members of Pastor Jones' church, we make a startling discovery: Every one of Pastor Jones' talents is equaled or surpassed by someone in the membership. A wealth of gifts lies buried because these talents are seemingly unneeded. True, no one in the church comes close to being a superstar like Pastor Jones. True also, for each talent there is probably a corresponding hang-up. But maybe God could tap those talents and heal those hang-ups if we thought differently about ministry.

What about the early church? Paul had a dramatic put-down for the superstar idea:

> *There are varieties of gifts, but the same Spirit. There are varieties of service, but the same Lord. There are many forms of work, but all of them, in everyone, are the work of the same God. In each of us the Spirit is manifested in one particular way, for some useful purpose. . . .*

For Christ is like a single body with its many limbs and organs, which, many as they are, together make up one body. . . .

A body is not one single organ, but many. Suppose the foot should say, "Because I am not a hand, I do not belong to the body," it does belong to the body none the less. . . . But, in fact, God appointed each limb and organ to its own place in the body, as he chose. If the whole were one single organ, there would not be a body at all; in fact, however, there are many different organs, but one body. . . .

Now you are Christ's body, and each of you a limb or organ of it. Within our community God has appointed, in the first place apostles, in the second place prophets, thirdly teachers; then miracle-workers, then those who have gifts of healing, or ability to help others or power to guide them, or the gift of ecstatic utterance of various kinds (1 Cor. 12:4-7, 12, 14-15, 18-20, 27-28, NEB).

Got that? "If the whole were one single organ, there would not be a body at all." If the pastor is a superstar then the church is an audience, not a body.

I had read many times what the Bible says about spiritual gifts. I never understood. I could not figure out why the whole thing really did not make any sense for the church *today.* It did not seem to fit. Could it really be that these words were written only for the early church, as some say?

Then it struck me. These words are for the church in every age, even if today they seem superfluous. For today we have all the gifts organized. We do not need the Spirit (dreadful thing to say!) to stir up gifts of ministry. We just need superstars to make the organization *Go.*

So we depend on our structures and our superstars. And we *know* the system *works*—just look at what the superstars are doing in their superchurches! We have the statistics and the buildings and the budgets to prove it. You can't argue with success.

There is only one problem.

There are not enough superstars to go around. Thousands of churches, but only hundreds of superstars.

Thank God for the superstars! They are of all people most fortunate. But the church of Jesus Christ cannot run on superstars any more than a horse can run on jet fuel. And God never intended that it should. There just are not that many superstars, actually or potentially, and there never will be. God does not promise the church an army of superstars. But he does promise to provide all necessary leadership through the gifts of the Spirit (Eph. 4:1-16). If a denomination must depend on pastoral superstars for growth, there is something drastically wrong with its structure and, more fundamentally, with its understanding of the church.

Pray the Lord of the harvest that he send forth reapers, not bosses.

Cheer up, discouraged pastor, discouraged "layman." The problem really is not your own inadequacy. Go reread the New Testament with a question: After Peter and Paul, where are the superstars? How did the early church "make it" without our organization, cathedrals or superstars?

Young Ralph C—— has been thinking of going into "the ministry" (not knowing he's already in it), but he hesitates because he knows he is not a superstar. (What if our churches did not require superstars?)

Chuck Y—— is 38 and has a good job with an electronics firm; I know him well. He is frustrated and would like some kind of expanded ministry—something more challenging than a Sunday school class. But he thinks he would have to quit his job and go to seminary first. (What if more pastors had secular employment and on-the-job training, as in the New Testament?)

Let's face it! James and John and Philip and Bartholomew could never have made it in the twentieth century. At least not within *our* churches. Neither would Epaphras, Mark, Priscilla, Aristarchus, Phoebe, Demas, Tryphosa, or Luke, some friends of Paul (Rom. 16, Philem. 23). These were no superstars in their day; they only look that way through the mists of history and tradition. But they were used of the Spirit, each according to their gifts. Their congregations had not heard that they had to have a superstar up front, so all believers worked together building up the community of faith. Many ministers in each congregation. Like a body, each part exercising its proper function.

Do our structures quench the Spirit?

"So, for the sake of your tradition, you make void the word of God" (Mt. 15:6). The Word of God is not bound—unless we bind it. What, then, does the unfettered Word say about the church?

It is time to go back to the Word to find a biblical ecclesiology, a biblical picture of the church that matches the new stirrings of the Spirit in our day.

Let both the Spirit *and* the Bride say, "Come!"

Biblical Material For New Wineskins

The Fellowship of the Holy Spirit

TRUE CHRISTIAN FELLOWSHIP—what the Greek New Testament calls *koinonia*—is the Spirit's gift to the church. Yet this fellowship is sadly lacking in much of the institutional church today. And this lack cuts to the heart of the impotence, rigidity and seeming irrelevance of much end-of-millennium Christianity.

The church is often attacked for its rigid institutionalism, its bloated bureaucracies, its "morphological fundamentalism." Critics call for more relevant structures and for a new ecclesiology. The New Testament concept of the *koinonia of the Holy Spirit* is the answer. It offers a key starting point in the quest for more intimate, less impersonal structures for the church's life.

A Fellowship Crisis

The church today is suffering a fellowship crisis. It is simply not experiencing nor demonstrating that "fellowship of the Holy Spirit" (2 Cor. 13:14) that marked the New Testament church. In a world of big, impersonal institutions, the church often looks like just another big, impersonal institution.

The church is highly organized just at the time when her members are caring less about organization and more about community. One seldom finds within the institutionalized church today that winsome intimacy among people where masks are dropped, honesty prevails and there is that sense of communication and community beyond the human—where there is literally the fellowship of and in the Holy Spirit.

A number of years ago Keith Miller put his finger precisely on this lack in his book, *The Taste of New Wine*. His words strike a responsive note, for people are still thirsty:

> *Our churches are filled with people who outwardly look con-*
> *tented and at peace but inwardly are crying out for someone*
> *to listen . . . just as they are—confused, frustrated, often*
> *frightened, guilty, and often unable to communicate even*
> *within their own families. But the other people in the church*
> *look so happy and contented that one seldom has the courage*
> *to admit his own deep needs before such a self-sufficient group*
> *as the average church meeting appears to be.*[1]

This unintentioned duplicity is an almost inevitable result of current institutional patterns of church organization. It is a description of the church without *koinonia*.

Koinonia is, of course, but one aspect of the church's total being. The New Testament church lived by worship, witness and fellowship. All these are essential for the church to be faithful. The church must preach and teach, and it must serve—following the example of Christ.

But *koinonia* is essential both for effective proclamation and for relevant serving. *Koinonia* is the church abiding in the vine, that it may bear much fruit. It is the Body becoming "joined and knit together," growing and maturing in love, so that the various gifts of the Spirit may be manifest in the world (Eph. 4:16). Often both the church's preaching and service have suffered simply for lack of true *koinonia*.

But what, specifically, is the *koinonia* of the Holy Spirit? And what does it tell us about church structure in our day?

What Is the "Fellowship of the Holy Spirit"?

In 2 Corinthians 13:14 Paul prays that "the fellowship [*koinonia*] of the Holy Spirit" may be with the Christian believers. And in Philippians 2:1 Paul speaks of the "fellowship [*koinonia*] of the Spirit" (AV).

Two dimensions are implied in these passages: the vertical dimension of believers' fellowship with God and the horizontal dimension of their *koinonia* together through the Holy Spirit. It is critical that these two aspects be held together and understood together. The New Testament idea of *koinonia* is not fully grasped until we see the significance of the horizontal and vertical dimensions *together*.

At first we may notice here only the vertical dimension of fellowship with God through the Holy Spirit. Isn't that what Paul is talking about? But the horizontal dimension is also very much present, and perhaps even primary: the fellowship among Christians which is the gift of the Spirit. As James Reid has written about 2 Corinthians 13:14, "This does not mean fellowship with the Spirit. It is a fellowship with God which he shares through the indwelling Spirit with those who are members of the body of Christ. *The fellowship of the Holy Spirit is the true description of the church.*"[2]

Much has been written about the meaning and implications of the word *koinonia*. Most of the discussion has emphasized the horizontal dimension, the fellowship of Christians with each other. But it is the vertical dimension that supplies the basic content to the whole idea of *koinonia*. *Koinonia* in the church must start with the fellowship of the Holy Spirit, or it lacks its New Testament dynamic. Hendrik Kraemer captures the core truth in his *Theology of the Laity:* "The fellowship *(koinonia)* with and in Jesus Christ and the Spirit is the creative ground and sustainer of the fellowship *(koinonia)* of the believers with each other."[3] The spiritual communion and fellowship in the church which truly is *koinonia* is something given by the Spirit; it is more than a function of our humanity. It partakes of the supernatural.

Two things, then, the fellowship of the Holy Spirit emphatically is *not:*

1. *It is not that superficial social fellowship which the very word* fellowship *often denotes in our churches today.* Such "fellowship" is generally no more supernatural than the weekly Kiwanis or Rotary meeting. Most of what passes for fellowship in the church—whatever its value—is something distinctly less than *koinonia*. It is "cheap fellowship," parallel to Bonhoeffer's "cheap grace." At best, it is a friendly fraternizing—appealing, but easily duplicated outside the church. Biblical *koinonia*, however, is unique to the church of Jesus Christ.

Typical church "fellowship" seldom reaches the level of *koinonia* because *koinonia* is neither understood, expected, nor sought. Consequently there are few or no suitable structures for *koinonia* in the church. The church has become accustomed to a pleasant, superficial sociality which is at best a cut-rate substitute for *koinonia*.

2. *On the other hand,* koinonia *is not simply some mystical communion that exists without reference to the structure of the church.* We may talk abstractly about "the fellowship of the church," as though it were something that automatically, and almost by definition, binds believers together. But the abstract concept is hollow apart from the actual gathering together of believers at a particular point in time and space. We cannot escape this, not on this earth. Christ himself emphasized the necessity of being together when he said, "Where two or three are gathered in my name, there am I in the midst of them" (Mt. 18:20). One can have fellowship with God when one is alone, and in any place, for God is spirit. *But one cannot normally have fellowship with another believer who is not present,* despite our mystical language. The fellowship of the Holy Spirit is not some ethereal power that spiritually binds believers together while they are physically apart. Rather, it is that deep spiritual community in Christ which believers experience when they come together as the church of Christ.

This is not to deny what Christians historically have called "the communion of saints." Sometimes in our prayer, and often in corporate worship, we may sense that larger mystical fellowship with "the whole company of heaven," the saints who have gone before.[4] This is also a gift from God. It is, however, the heavenly counterpart of what we are to experience *daily* as we really are together face to face, as flesh-and-blood parts of the Body of Christ.

More positively, we can describe the fellowship of the Holy Spirit in the following terms:

1. *The* koinonia *of the Holy Spirit is that fellowship among believers which the Holy Spirit gives.* It is precisely that experience of a deeper communion, of a supernatural intercommunication, that perhaps every believer occasionally experiences in the presence of other believers.[5] Its basis is the oneness that Christians share in Christ. A shared faith, a shared salvation and a shared divine nature are the roots of *koinonia*. The basic idea of the word *koinonia* is, in fact, that of something held in common—shared life.

2. *It is the fellowship of Christ with his disciples.* Jesus spent over three years living and working in fellowship together with a small

group of disciples. As Robert Coleman notes, "He actually spent more time with His disciples than with everybody else in the world put together. He ate with them, slept with them, and talked with them for the most part of His entire active ministry."[6] These disciples not only learned from Christ; they shared a depth of community that was the prototype of the *koinonia* of the early church. It is interesting that in the midst of Christ's important discourse during the Last Supper three disciples felt free to interrupt with comments or questions (Jn. 14:5, 8, 22). Together they were experiencing the fellowship of the Holy Spirit.[7]

3. *It is the fellowship of the early church,* as recorded in the book of Acts. The first Christians knew an unusual unity, oneness of purpose, common love and mutual sharing—in other words, *koinonia.* This was more than either the immediate joy of conversion or the solidarity of shared beliefs. It was an atmosphere, a spiritual environment that grew among the first believers as they prayed, learned and worshiped together in their own homes (Acts 2:42-46; 5:42).

4. *It is the earthly counterpart and foretaste of the eternal fellowship of heaven.* The joy of heaven is the freedom of eternal communion with God and fellow believers, without physical limitations. As the earthly model of this heavenly reality, *koinonia* in the church shares the same spiritual nature as life in heaven; it is not qualitatively different. But it suffers the necessary limitations of the flesh and of space and time. Thus *koinonia* in the church is neither continuous nor universal. Rather, it is interrupted, partial, local—necessarily so. It is limited and affected by physical factors, but its essential reality is not of this world.

5. *It is analogous to the unity, fellowship and communion between Christ and the Father.* A parallel exists between the communion of the Trinity and the *koinonia* of believers among themselves and with God. Christ's prayer in John 17 is especially suggestive here. Jesus asks that his disciples "may be one, as we are one." More generally, he prays for all future Christians that they all "may be one, Father, just as you are in me and I in you. May they also be in us so that the world may believe that you have sent me" (Jn. 17 :11, 21, NIV). *Koinonia* is the fulfillment of this prayer in the church and thus a manifestation in space and time of the communion of the Holy Trinity. It is a supernatural intersharing

between the Persons of the Godhead and the church on earth, inseparably involving both the vertical and horizontal dimensions. Christ wanted his followers to be one in their *koinonia*—one not only with God but also with each other.

Such *koinonia* is the gift of the Holy Spirit. But is the church then powerless to create or nurture this fellowship? Or may church structures provide the conditions for the fellowship of the Holy Spirit?

Daniel J. Fleming makes the following point in his book *Living as Comrades:* "The fashioning and preservation of this *koinonia* . . . is the peculiar work of the Holy Spirit. But . . . we can help or hinder that consummation by the degree to which we consciously endeavor to enter into community with fellow human beings."[8] And that applies to the church as well as to each believer.

The Bible is largely silent as to specific structures for the church. The New Testament contains no Sinai revelation as to the "pattern of the tabernacle." We are free to create those structures most conducive to the mission and need of the church in our time, within the broad outlines of the biblical vision of the church.[9] The very idea of the *koinonia* of the Holy Spirit may have something very significant to say about such structures.

Implications for Church Structure

At Pentecost the Holy Spirit gave the infant church, among other things, the gift of *koinonia*. This is the only explanation for the early Christian community described in Acts. The creation of genuine fellowship is an integral part of the work of the Holy Spirit. In this sense the Holy Spirit's work in each believer cannot be separated from what he is doing in the whole church—the church not as so many separate believers but precisely as a community of faith.

Failure to see this vital interconnection between the individual and group aspects of the Spirit's working weakens our understanding both of the individual believer and of the church. It is, first, to view believers' spiritual development in too much of an individualized, separated sense, as though Christians grow best in isolation. And second, it misses an element of basic significance for the structure and ministry of the church: The church provides the context for spiritual growth by sharing together a fellowship which is at once the gift of the Spirit and the environment in which the Spirit may operate.

Thus a natural connection links the fellowship of the Holy Spirit to church structure. The nature of this *koinonia* in fact contains several implications for the form of the church.

First of all, as already noted, the fellowship of the Holy Spirit is a function of the church gathered, not of the church scattered. The obvious implication for church structure: *The church must make sufficient provision to be gathered together if it is to experience koinonia. Koinonia* requires being together in one place at one time under the direction of the Holy Spirit. We can talk about the fellowship of the Holy Spirit as being solely a spiritual reality, ignoring the space-time limitations, but this is meaningless. The fact is that the fellowship of the Holy Spirit—New Testament *koinonia* in the church—*requires,* as an *absolute necessity,* physical proximity. The church does not experience the fellowship of the Holy Spirit if it does not meet together in an atmosphere conducive to the Spirit's working.

Second, the fellowship of the Holy Spirit naturally suggests communication. Communion without communication would be a contradiction in terms. Thus a second implication for church structure: *The church must meet together in ways that permit and encourage communication among the members.*

This fact immediately raises questions about most traditional structures of worship. Whatever its value, the traditional church worship service is not well designed for intercommunication, for fellowship. It is designed, both by liturgy and architecture, principally for a one-way kind of communication, pulpit-to-pew. Indeed, communication between two worshipers during the church services is considered rude, outside the spirit of worship. As Alan Watts commented caustically, "Participants sit in rows looking at the back of each other's necks, and are in communication only with the leader."[10]

The traditional church service is usually not the best structure for experiencing the fellowship of the Holy Spirit. In fact, no church meeting is conducive to *koinonia* if it is based on one-way, leader-to-group communication—whether it be prayer meeting, Sunday school class or Bible study hour. *Koinonia* appears and flourishes only in structures that allow and encourage communication.

And since *koinonia* involves the vertical dimension as well as the horizontal, this communication also implies communion with God. In other words, prayer is part of *koinonia.*

A third implication for wineskins involves the element of freedom. Paul gives us the principle, "Where the Spirit of the Lord is, there is freedom" (2 Cor. 3:17). The Holy Spirit is the liberator, the freer. The freedom of the Spirit and the *koinonia* of the Spirit go together. Where there is *koinonia* there is also freedom and openness, an atmosphere which permits "speaking the truth in love" (Eph. 4:15). True *koinonia* can be experienced only where there is such freedom of the Spirit.

The implication for structure: *The church must provide structures which are sufficiently informal and intimate to permit the freedom of the Spirit.* There must be a sense of the unexpected and the unprogrammed when believers come together, the excitement of the unpredictable, a freedom from set patterns and forms. Frequently in an informal and rather loosely structured gathering of believers one finds a greater openness to God's moving and thus a greater likelihood that the fellowship of the Holy Spirit will be experienced.

This is not, of course, to argue against proper planning, form and liturgy. Believers need those times of solemn corporate worship in which the High and Holy God is honored with dignity and reverence. But in the midst of the dignity and reverence many a lonely believer inwardly cries out for the warm, healing touch of *koinonia*. Believers need to know by experience that the Most High God is also the Most Nigh God (Is. 57:15). If traditional corporate worship is not regularly supplemented with informal opportunities for *koinonia,* believers easily drift into a practical deism while the church becomes the sacred guardian of a powerless form of godliness—the solemn preserver of empty wineskins. On the other hand, form and liturgy take on new meaning for Christians who are living and growing in *koinonia*.

Robert Raines makes essentially the same point in his book *New Life in the Church:*

> *The church must foster and sustain the conditions in which koinonia can be known. This cannot be done for most people simply through morning worship. Worship is indispensable as the weekly meeting of the Christian community. But it is effective only as the total sharing of all the people of the friendship in Christ they have known between Sundays.*[11]

Finally, the fellowship of the Holy Spirit suggests a learning situation. Jesus said that when the Holy Spirit came he would "teach you everything, and remind you of all that I have said to you" (Jn. 14:26). He would testify of Christ and guide the believers into new truth (Jn. 15:26; 16: 13). The Holy Spirit came to teach, to reveal the Word.

Since it is the same Spirit of God who inbreathes and speaks through the Holy Scriptures (2 Tim. 3:16; 1 Pet. 1:21), and since these Scriptures themselves testify of Christ (Jn. 5:39), it follows that the *koinonia* of the Holy Spirit is naturally related to Bible study. We in fact find the two themes connected in the early church, which devoted itself "to the apostles' teaching and *koinonia*" (Acts 2:42).

The key implication here: *Church structure must provide for Bible study in the context of community.* When Christians meet jointly with the objective task of Bible study before them and under the guidance of the Holy Spirit, they experience *koinonia* that has life-changing results. They are touched by the Spirit and the Word. They find that the way to learn of Christ is in the environment of a community of believers taught by the Holy Spirit.

The idea of the *koinonia* of the Holy Spirit, then, suggests that the church should provide structures in which (1) believers gather together, (2) intercommunication is encouraged, (3) an informal atmosphere allows the freedom of the Spirit, and (4) direct Bible study is central.

Most contemporary church patterns and structures clearly do not meet these criteria. But there is one structure that does: some form of small group. *The* koinonia *of the Holy Spirit is most likely to be experienced when Christians meet together informally in small-group fellowships.*

The small group can meet the above criteria. It brings believers together at one point in time and space. Its smallness and intimacy allow a high degree of communion and intercommunication. It does not require formal structuring; it can maintain order without stifling the informality and openness conducive to the freedom of the Spirit. And finally, it offers an ideal context for in-depth Bible study.

In first-century Greco-Roman culture, a *koinonia* was a voluntary partnership or association for mutual support and common tasks. The first Christians adapted this social form for Gospel purposes, becoming the *koinonia* of the Spirit.[12] We can learn from their experience and their creativity.

The early church experienced this *koinonia* of the Holy Spirit. We know also that the early Christians met together in small groups in homes. Coincidence? Or does the very idea of the *koinonia* of the Holy Spirit not suggest the need for some kind of small group fellowships as a basic structure within the church?

George Webber in his discussion of small groups in *The Congregation in Mission* notes, "No relationship of love can develop unless there are structures in which it can grow."[13] *Koinonia* in the Holy Spirit grows when there are structures to nourish it.

The People of God

ANOTHER PERSPECTIVE FOR viewing the church is to see it as the result of God's cosmic purpose in calling and preparing a special people. This also relates to wineskins.

Adam and Eve were to "be fruitful and multiply, and fill the earth," becoming a people (Gen. 1:28).[1] God's promise to Abraham was, "I will make of you a great nation" (Gen. 12:2)—and he did. God chose the children of Israel, redeeming them from Egypt, saying, "I will take you as my people, and I will be your God" (Ex. 6:7; compare Dt. 7:6). This theme echoes consistently through the Old Testament.

Moving into the New Testament, we learn that the people of God finds its center and basis in Jesus Christ. The unfaithfulness of God's people in the Old Testament did not thwart God's plan. God is still calling out and preparing his people, not principally the biological Israel but the new and true Israel, the church.[2] John the Baptist came in "the spirit and power of Elijah," his ministry "to make ready a people prepared for the Lord" (Lk. 1:17).

Paul was deeply conscious of God's plan to prepare a people on the basis of faith. Christ "gave himself for us that he might redeem us from all iniquity and purify for himself a people of his own who are zealous for good deeds" (Tit. 2:14; compare Rom. 9:25-26; 2 Cor. 6:16). The same fact is cited by James (Acts 15:14), John (Rev. 21:3) and the writer to the Hebrews (Heb. 8:10). Peter says, "You are a chosen race, a royal priesthood, a holy nation, God's own people. . . . Once you were not a people, but now you are God's people; once you had not received mercy, but now you have received mercy" (1 Pet. 2:9-10). This is the "new covenant" of which Jeremiah spoke, in which God says, "I will be their God, and they shall be my people" (Jer. 31:33).

But precisely what does it mean, biblically, to be a people? And how should the church be structured in order to experience this reality of peoplehood?

The Biblical Basis

The idea of a *people* has rich biblical and especially Old Testament roots. Biblical Greek uses the word *laos* to refer to the church as a people. This word (from which we get "laity") occurs over 2,000 times in the Septuagint (the Greek Old Testament), usually translating the Hebrew word *'am*. *Laos* is the word commonly used for Israel as God's people; "it serves to emphasize the special and privileged religious position of this people as the people of God."[3] In the Old Testament, *laos* "is the national society of Israel according to its religious basis and distinction."[4]

In the New Testament, *laos* occurs some 140 times. It is the word both Paul and Peter use to describe the church as *a people*, the new Israel. Thus in the New Testament "a new and figurative Christian concept arises along with the old biological and historical view and crowds it out."[5]

This forming of a people provides the basis for the church's mission of service and proclamation. *As a people, the church is itself the verification of the message it proclaims,* or else the betrayal of that message. As John Howard Yoder notes, "The work of God is the calling of a people, whether in the Old Covenant or the New. . . . That men and women are called together to a new social wholeness is itself the work of God, which gives meaning to history, from which both personal conversion . . . and missionary instrumentalities are derived."[6] Yoder continues,

> *Pragmatically it is self-evident that there can be no procedure of proclamation without a community, distinct from the rest of society, to do the proclaiming. Pragmatically it is just as clear that there can be no evangelistic call . . . into a new kind of fellowship and learning, if there is not such a body of persons, again distinct from the totality of society, [that people can be a part of]. . . . If it is not the case that there are in a given place people of various characters and origins who have been brought together in Jesus Christ, then there is not in that place the new humanity and in*

that place the gospel is not true. If, on the other hand, this miracle of new creation has occurred, then all the verbalizations and inter-pretations whereby this body communicates to the world around it are simply explications of . . . its presence.[7]

The church is constituted a people just as any person is con-stituted a child of God—by grace through faith in Jesus Christ. The converted person becomes part of a transformed people. And the working out of this reality always produces a church with New Testament dynamic, unless stifled by unbiblical traditions.

Biblically, we can distinguish at least five characteristics of the people of God:

1. *The church is a chosen people.* The accent here is on God's sov-ereignty and initiative. It is God who moves to choose and form a people for himself. The church is the result of God's sovereign grace (2 Tim. 1:9). It exists because God has acted graciously in history.

The fact of God's choosing a people for himself implies a distinction between those who are chosen and those who are not. If God has chosen a people, then that people *really exists as a people,* in some sense identifiable and distinct from the world. It is not an anonymous people.

2. *The church is a pilgrim people.* Here we have a theme that is difficult but biblically necessary. Difficult, because it can be mis-construed to mean theological and practical withdrawal from the world. But necessary, because without this emphasis the church slips into the worst kind of worldliness.

Adam and Eve were not created to be pilgrims. God made a home for them that should have been permanent: "The LORD God planted a garden in Eden, in the east; and there he put the man whom he had formed" (Gen. 2:8). Adam and Eve were at home in the world and in harmony with their environment—morally, physically and psychologically. This was the original ecology of God's creation.

But when sin entered Adam and Eve became wanderers. Our first parents were expelled from the garden. After his act of murder, Cain was condemned to be "a fugitive and a wanderer on the earth" (Gen. 4:12). But what happened? "Cain went away from the presence of the LORD, . . . and he built a city" (Gen. 4:16-17). The world came under the dominion of evil, and humanity tried to build a substitute Eden in this tainted world.[8]

So henceforth the story of redemption is the story of God's *calling out* a people for himself. This people is called to be pilgrims, to live in active tension with the world, "looking for a city not made with hands," knowing that the time of final reconciliation, the end of the pilgrimage, will come.

The church is a pilgrim people, "resident aliens."[9] This does not mean that it is completely divorced from, or has no responsibility for, its cultural context. Quite the opposite. The church's mission is still reconciliation. It does mean, however, a fundamental moral tension between the church and human society. The pilgrim aspect results from the estrangement produced by sin. It reminds us of the alienation between humans and their world. Yet this is a necessary precondition for true reconciliation.

3. *The church is a covenant people.* The relationship between God and his people is specific and is morally and ethically based. It is grounded in the covenant, which means the church constantly faces the challenge of fidelity or infidelity to covenant provisions.

A major significance of the covenant is that it grounds God's people in real history. The covenant implies a *covenant event* in which the contract between God and humanity was actually established in space and time. The Hebrews were deeply conscious of this. Thus we have the historical giving of the law in the Old Testament and the establishing of the new covenant in the historical Last Supper, death and resurrection of Jesus Christ. The covenant is established in historical occurrences that can be recorded, commemorated, and reviewed.

These historical events have been recorded for us in the Scriptures; hence, the Bible is the church's Book of the Covenant. The people of God is a people "under the Word." The Bible is normative for the life of the church, not because of some particular doctrine of inspiration but precisely because it is the Book of the Covenant.[10]

4. *The church is a witness people.* Its task is to point to that which has happened in the past and is happening in the present which is truly the action of God. The church must be able to say "This is That," says Jess Moody. It must have something miraculous to

point to. If our only success "is that which can be explained in terms of organization and management—that is, something the world could do with the same expenditure of effort and technique, the world will one day finally repudiate us."[11]

The church must witness to God's personal acts throughout history—and, as the book of Acts makes clear, supremely to the resurrection of Jesus Christ (for example, Acts 2:32, 3:15, 4:33). It must also be able to point to the contemporary miracles of personal conversion, genuine community, and servant living which give credence to the miracles of an earlier day. As Yoder emphasizes,

> *The political novelty which God brings into the world is a community of those who serve instead of ruling, who suffer instead of inflicting suffering, whose fellowship crosses social lines instead of reinforcing them. This new Christian community . . .is not only a vehicle of the gospel or fruit of the gospel;* it is the good news.[12]

But this witness is not a purely passive one. God has given the church a "ministry of reconciliation" that "through the church" God might bring about the reconciliation of "all things . . . , things in heaven and things on earth" (2 Cor. 5:18; Eph. 3:10, 1:10; Col. 1:20). This gives Christians a mandate for working in various ministries of reconciliation, performing those "good works, which God prepared beforehand" for the fulfilling of his plan of reconciliation (Eph. 2:10).

5. *Finally, the church is a holy people.* The biblical demand for holiness is insistent: "You shall be holy for I am holy" (See, for example, Lev. 11:44-45,19:2, 20:7; 1 Pet. 1:15-16.) Says Paul, Christ sanctifies the church that it may be "without a spot or wrinkle or any thing of the kind . . . so that she may be holy and without blemish" (Eph. 5:27).

This holiness is a sharing of the divine nature (2 Pet. 1:4). It is the fruit of the Spirit dwelling and acting, not only within each believer but within the redeemed community. It is an aspect of the fellowship of the Holy Spirit. Human personality and Christian community were made to be saturated with the Spirit of God, and reach their potential only when they are.

Implications for Church Structure

Theologically, the church is God's special people, but in fact it often fails to live up to this high calling. Whatever the so-called spiritual reasons for this lack, it must also be seen as a problem of ecclesiology, and specifically of church structure. What can the church do to incarnate this reality, to demonstrate it visibly? It seems to me that four implications are key:

First, each believer must be able to feel himself or herself a part of the larger organic unity of the people of God. This means *the church must meet together in a way that encourages and expresses its peoplehood.* It is meaningless to talk of peoplehood if in fact our structures stifle the experiencing of this reality.

Here again we must remember the temporal obstacles which, in this life, believers face—obstacles that keep our sense of peoplehood from being realized. There are mystics, of course, who enjoy an isolated existence and do feel, mystically, their union with other Christians. But their experience is far from the reality of most of us, nor is it the ideal. The average Christian needs church structures which lead to a sense of peoplehood.

But what kinds of structures build this kind of peoplehood? Obviously, structures which actually bring the people of God together at specific points in space and time. So this suggests a second guideline for church structure: *The church must meet together regularly as a large congregation.* It must actually come together as a people.

This is one reason why small-group fellowships, essential as they are, are not by themselves sufficient to sustain the life of the church. Each cell of the Body of Christ must see and feel its unity with the larger body.

It is not physically possible, of course, to bring the entire Body of Christ together at one time and place. Physical limitations require intermediate structures—whether associations, denominations or movements—that bring together a large cross section of the people of God, where the homogeneity is not social or political or economic, but spiritual.

The need for such large-group structures was first brought home to me when we lived in Brazil. In the city of São Paulo the fiery Pentecostal evangelist Manoel de Mello was building what was said to be the largest church sanctuary in the world. In a previously completed part of this temple thousands of his follow-ers in the "Brasil Para Cristo" movement would come together each Saturday night. Packing into public buses, perhaps singing as they came, they converged on their center. From all parts of the city and outlying areas they came, ready to share the joy and excitement of a great throng of believers. Together they would pray, sing, witness and hear their leader. Later they would be scattered in hundreds of congregations around the city, many of them small and struggling. But they were not discouraged: They knew they were a part of a people, a movement! Something was happening, something big, something God-sized. They had seen it and felt it.

Some might scoff, speaking of "emotional release" and "crowd psychology." Certainly there are the dangers of extremes and counterfeits. But we should recognize the essential human depen-dence on structures that is a part of our humanity while we are bound in space and time. And one cannot deny the practical value of this identification with one's church as a people.

Actually, most new religious movements have instinctively sensed, in the beginning, the need for some form of regular large-group gatherings—mass rallies, evangelistic campaigns, congresses, or whatever. Often mass preaching services, such as in early Methodism, fulfilled this function. Many of the large churches in Korea, such as the Yoido Full Gospel Church and Kwanglim Methodist Church, have a keen sense of this dynamic of peoplehood.

There are different models, however. A variety of forms is possible. The essential thing is gathering together a large group of believers on a regular and frequent basis—the periodic uniting of smaller congregations and cells into a great throng.

Further, taking our cue in part from the Old Testament, we may stress the need for *covenant experiences*. Both the ancient Hebrews and the early Christians were conscious of being a people *because something had happened*. God had acted in history to choose and form a people. In the Old Testament these acts of God were periodically recalled by special festivals and celebrations. Such commemorations were covenant experiences, occasions for the remembrance and renewal of the covenant between God and his people. And this suggests a third implication for church structure: *The church needs periodic festivals which have covenant significance.*

I am not talking about superficial celebrations patterned after those of the world. Rather, I mean occasions which spring from and celebrate the genuine joy and excitement of corporately sharing the fact that God has acted. This is what the Old Testament religious festivals were all about. The church needs festivals analogous to the Day of Atonement and the Feast of Tabernacles, not analogous to the Tournament of Roses, New Year's Eve or the Super Bowl!

Interestingly enough, many American Protestants used to have such a festival—the camp meeting. In the best camp meetings, whether denominational or nondenominational, the sense of peoplehood and covenant responsibility was periodically and powerfully recaptured. Thousands flocked to such meetings during much of the nineteenth century.[13]

But the camp meeting has gradually faded into the mists of American folk history or been replaced by the family camp, and no suitable substitute has yet appeared. Billy Graham crusades, large rallies of the Vineyard and other movements, and more recently regional Cell Church conferences have on occasion sparked some sense of peoplehood, but only sporadically; their main purpose lies elsewhere.

Whatever the form of such covenant experiences, they should fulfill four main functions, at least:

1. *Celebration of the acts of God:* Reciting with joy and praise God's acts in biblical history, in Jesus Christ (especially the incarnation, resurrection and Pentecost) and in the history of this particular subgroup of God's people.

Some of the Psalms recount in historical sequence God's dealings with his people. These psalms were probably used in large worship assemblies. Why shouldn't the church today hold periodic "covenant celebrations," picking up where these psalms leave off and recounting God's dealings down through church history? Certainly the acts of God are discernible in various movements and people, and these can legitimately be celebrated, giving glory to God.[14]

2. *Covenant renewal:* Reciting the terms of God's covenant with us, both God's part and ours. This would of necessity involve repentance, confession and rededication to God as well as a renewed sense of fidelity to the Bible as the written Word and Book of the Covenant.

100

3. *Evaluation and definition.* Evaluation: Have we been faithful to the covenant? Where have we failed? What changes should be made? Have we betrayed the biblical perspective either through pickling our faith in unbiblical traditions or through making changes that are equally unbiblical in their inspiration? And definition: What does it mean, today, to be the people of God? What is our relationship to non-Christian culture? What are the limits of our engagement with the world?

4. *Renewal of a vision for the future.* Where there is no vision, the people perish. We must think historically and biblically about the future. We must catch a vision of future possibilities, remembering we serve a God who yet promises to do a new thing. Covenant occasions are right for the continuing definition of a biblical eschatology.

All of the foregoing brings us to a final implication of the concept of the people of God for church structure. As we have seen, the people of God does not exist for nothing or by accident. The basis of the church's existence as a people is all-important. Therefore, *in the church's structuring of itself the basis of the church's existence as a people must be kept central.*

What is this basis of the people of God? It is nothing other than *the Word of God*—God-in-relationship, the Person of Jesus Christ as living and active and the Bible as historically conditioned but once-for-all revealed truth (Heb. 4:12-13). The church is constituted a people by the Word of God.

Here, perhaps, is where large-group and small-group structures fit together. The small group is an excellent context for Bible study and genuine theological work by the whole Body of Christ, rather than by professional theologians. Here the real biblical meaning of being the people of God in these days needs to be hammered out.

For some, it is an offense to speak of the church as a distinct people. For those who wish to emphasize the solidarity of the whole human race in the face of injustice and other social ills, any suggestion that the church is or ought to be a distinct people is scandalous. But the fact remains that the Bible speaks in these terms. Further, the church as a distinct community is a practical necessity, as we have already pointed out. Truth does not exist independently of persons, and persons do not exist independently of structures of common life.

But how does one define who is and who is not a part of the people of God? What are the criteria for identification? Various answers might be given, but this much is clear: The kind of structures suggested here, which heighten and define the Church's sense of peoplehood, naturally tend to draw together genuine believers and repel those not sincerely interested in the things of the Spirit.

Where church structure is functional, where wineskins allow and encourage the sense of being the people of God rather than quench the Spirit, there we may hope for a new depth of Christian faithfulness and for new life in the church.

The Mind of Christ

WE LIVE IN a world increasingly hostile to all that is truly human. Though we hear much talk of expanded consciousness, sensitivity training, new forms of community and the like, fundamental forces are moving to undermine the uniqueness of being human. When we strip away the jargon, we often find an unvoiced conviction that, fundamentally, a man or a woman is nothing more than a machine or a complex of chemicals. The human mind is merely "a slow-clockrate modified digital machine, with multiple distinguishable parallel processing, all working in salt water."[1]

But the church is to know the mind of Christ, the renewed image of God. In a high-tech age, this is revolutionary.

"We have the mind of Christ," says Paul in 1 Corinthians 2:16. And again, "Let the same mind be in you that was in Christ Jesus" (Phil. 2:5). These statements reveal two things: The character of Jesus Christ is the standard for the church, and there is a unique aspect of Christ's character—what Paul here calls "mind"—which the community of God's people must experience.

It is this very aspect of Christ's character which is most threatened in godless contemporary society. But here also we find material for new wineskins.

The Uniqueness of the Mind of Christ

The characteristic word for "mind" in the New Testament is *nous*. This Greek word appears twenty-four times, twenty-one of them in Paul's writings. "Mind" in the New Testament, however, does not have the technical sense the word acquired in Greek philosophy. The New Testament usage is closer to the idea of "heart" in the Old Testament.[2]

Without going into a technical study of *nous* and related words, we may say that when the New Testament speaks of mind it is referring to the totality of the human person as a rational, moral and spiritual being. We are confronted here with the uniqueness of human personality—with the image of God. We meet *personhood*. This shows the relationship of statements such as "we have the mind of Christ" to declarations like "those whom he foreknew he also predestined to be conformed to the image of his Son" (Rom. 8:29). Christians, restored to relationship with God through Christ in conversion, can have the mind of Christ because they were created in the image of God.

The image of God makes man and woman unique in a world of things, animals and machines. Jesus Christ, "the image of the invisible God" (Col. 1:15), came to conquer sin and restore that image. He atoned for sin and founded the church. And God's express will for the church is that "all of us come to the unity of the faith and of the knowledge of the Son of God, to maturity, to the measure of the full stature of Christ" (Eph. 4:13). This is to incarnate the mind of Christ in the church of God.

But what is the image of God in us? What is the uniqueness of the mind of Christ? Essentially, it is the freedom to respond to God, to enter into love-community with him and, thus, with other persons. This uniqueness will naturally be seen somewhat differently in different ages and cultures. In the context of today's high-tech society, however, it especially means five things. These are key elements of the mind of Christ in the church today—elements which were clearly demonstrated in the personality and character of Jesus Christ and are thus significant for the church, his Body.

1. *Spontaneity.* Spontaneity is basic to personality. Art, love and play all presuppose the freedom to be spontaneous—to do the unnecessary, the unplanned, the unrequired. Spontaneity is the unpredictability of Jesus, who failed to fit anyone's mold. Spontaneity is the creative in man and woman, the capacity and impulse to act freely. As Mildred Wynkoop observes, "The very fact of difference and unpredictability" gives human beings a unique value.[3]

But spontaneity is the death of technique. Spontaneity is outlawed in the world of technology—it is too dangerous. The worst sin of a machine or a computer is to be unpredictable.

Predictability is understandable when we are dealing with machines. But today the complexity of modern society requires the increasing use of machines to regulate and monitor human behavior. And this is accompanied by the growth of effective means for controlling society through a technology of human behavior. Futurologists Kahn and Wiener wrote,

> *The modern industrial society is highly differentiated and therefore requires great integration in order to function. . . .*
>
> *Greater wealth and improved technology give us a wider range of alternatives; but once an alternative has been chosen, much regulation and imposed order is needed. Thus with geometric increase in the complexity and organization of modern life, corresponding . . . increases in the scope and complexity of human and organization controls will become necessary. One need not assume the triumph of the police mentality . . . to foresee this. Each restriction will have its valid and attractive rationale, which may even be libertarian.*[4]

In other words, the more complicated society becomes, the more people must be regulated. "No Parking" signs were unnecessary before cars, and pollution controls were not needed before the Industrial Revolution.

In technological society, spontaneity may become the true test of freedom—spontaneity, not in the sense of a "freedom" to turn inward to a self-indulgent irrationalism (which is no real freedom and produces no effective action in the world), but the freedom to create, to act, to love in ways that produce and change human relationships and social structures. Yet this very spontaneity, unique to human personality and enabled by the Holy Spirit, is threatened by technological society.

2. *Individuality.* Each human being is a unique person. All people have value because they are created and loved by God. Therefore something unquantifiable is found in man and woman. Human beings can be counted, but only by ignoring what is most uniquely human.

Since people are created in God's image they have value *because they are,* regardless of what they can do. If human beings do not share the uniqueness of God's infinity, they most certainly share the dimension of personality—to borrow a thought from Francis Schaeffer.[5]

Technological society, of course, is not ultimately interested in what is unique in each person but rather in what is identical— what can be counted, standardized, computerized, manipulated. And the increasing sophistication of behavioral technology greatly broadens the range of the quantifiable. Already advanced technological societies have moved far beyond the mere quantification of income, education, employment, residence, credit standing and the like, and are moving into records of religious beliefs, political preferences, mental health and personality types. Some are even seeking a quantifiable index to the quality of life.[6]

Alvin Toffler argues that advanced technology tends toward diversification rather than standardization.[7] This may well be where technology eventually leads, but such diversification is not an unmixed blessing. Technology gradually reaches such a sophisticated level that it is able to subdivide people according to increasingly limited criteria, with the end in view of attaining a particular result. In the United States, the result has been "the niching of America."[8] It is superficial therefore to equate technological diversity with greater freedom, as Toffler seems to do. Rather, diversification facilitates manipulation. This is in fact the goal, though it is seldom stated so baldly.

All manipulation is a threat to real personality—and hence to true spirituality. In the church, manipulation produces a synthetic religion in which religious "experience" is technically induced and maintained. The believer becomes object, not subject; an "it," not an "I." We need a healthy fear today of any tendency to reduce evangelism and religious experience to mere technology.

Because Jesus Christ died for each person, not just for "humanity," and because he saw worth in each person and treated everyone so, the Christian church must never lose the biblical emphasis on individuality. In the face of the quantification of society and the manipulation of people, Christians must insist that individuality is a gift from God and an integral part of the mind of Christ.

3. *Moral sense.* Even without the light of the Bible, people distinguish between right and wrong, good and evil.[9] This moral awareness is a dimension of the image of God. Through the Scriptures we understand that the question is not, however, fundamentally one of right and wrong, not a matter of morality and moral codes. Essentially, our moral sense is our awareness that we are responsible beings before the Creator-God. God exists and creates; therefore every person, created in the divine image, is responsible (and response-able) before him. In this relationship of responsibility we find the meaning of life.

But what happens to morality in a high-tech world? Two things. First, the moral sense is blunted through the eclipse of ultimate meaning. Industrialization and urbanization break down traditional worldviews with their accompanying mores and place society in flux. A general wave of "immorality" and the "breakdown of moral standards" follows. When this occurs in a society heavily influenced by the Christian faith, the result is a general rejection of Christian morality and the kind of moral degeneration now evident in the United States and Western Europe.

People cannot live long in a moral vacuum, however. They must have a morality. And technology expands to fill the vacuum, for technology brings its own morality. This is the second thing that happens to morality in a high-tech world. Technology is concerned with means, not ultimately with ends. What is technologically feasible (the means) is good in itself, and the question of ends becomes superfluous. Though some voices question the identification of technology with progress, the march of technology itself is able, in the long run, to quiet these protests. Technological progress is good in itself (better cars and TVs, better detergents and cleaners, more space exploration). And even when techniques are perceived as not necessarily good, we discover they are essential for survival (antipollution controls, the pill, new techniques of surveillance, better bombs, computerized information banks and so on). And how can what is essential for survival be doubted?

Thus technology produces its own moral values—what Jacques Ellul calls "technological morality." This new morality, says Ellul, "tends to bring human behavior into harmony with the technological world, to set up a new scale of values in terms of technology, and to create new virtues."[10] Technology itself will provide the means for instilling such a morality and winning adherence to it. For, says Ellul,

> . . . *the techniques of psychology will be able to reach into [the] heart itself, to personalize the objective reasons for the behavior, to obtain through technical procedures loyalty and good will, joy itself in the carrying out of the "duty," which like everything else ceases to be painful and exhausting in the comfortable world of techniques.*[11]

B. F. Skinner pointed the way to such an induced morality twenty-five years ago. He argued that morality is, after all, no more than "a problem in human behavior." How people feel morally therefore "is a question for which a science of behavior should have an answer."[12] Behavioral technology will, when called upon, engineer a morality to match the social need.

Such a technological morality is antithetical to the Christian faith, not because the specific behavior induced would be "immoral"—it might, in fact, be highly commendable—but because it is a morality of means, not of ends; of technological necessity, not of personal relationships with God and others. It is a morality on the level of things and non-conscious being, not on the high level of conscious persons. The social behavior of ants may be quite decorous, but it is not for that reason an adequate model for human morality.

The church, however, is called upon to deepen our moral capacity and give it meaning through Christ-centered relationships, both horizontal and vertical. This is an essential part of the meaning of discipleship. The church is in danger of an insidious worldliness at this point. For all its professed interest in persons, too often the institutional church betrays itself in the way it actually treats people. Our moral sense—given as a capacitor for true, loving and holy relationships—can all too easily be manipulated by "spiritual" techniques to keep people in line. A warning to a small child to be quiet in church because she is in God's house, besides being bad theology, can be simply a technique to induce desired behavior. This is but one small example of what often happens on a much larger scale.

4. *Self-consciousness.* Human beings, as Francis Schaeffer has noted, are unique in that "in a very real way [they live inside their] own head."[13] The Psalms repeatedly speak of this interior life—that life which only the person knows and whose depths go deeper than our own consciousness and are known only to God. This reflects the image of God and is essential to the formation of the mind of Christ in us.

Many things in the world either develop, distort or deaden self-consciousness. Most of what comes through television and films actually has such a deadening effect, as do alcohol and many kinds of drugs. Many forms of non-Christian mysticism tend in the same direction: the swallowing up of one's own self-consciousness in a transpersonal, universal Whole. In George Orwell's *1984* the development of "Newspeak" was actually intended to limit consciousness and eliminate choice, thus reducing behavior from a rational to an instinctual level: "Orthodoxy is unconsciousness."[14]

In a world that tends to reduce our self-awareness, or to treat it as a mere evolutionary quirk legitimately subject to behavioral engineering, the church of Jesus Christ must never forget that self-consciousness is a gift from God. Therefore self-consciousness should be affirmed, not as self-preoccupation or the basis for a morbid spiritual introspection but as the indispensable foundation for communication, for love, for volition, and hence for worship. Self-consciousness is essential for true freedom.

5. *Volition.* The Bible speaks constantly of the will of God. Jesus said, "I have come . . . not to do my own will, but the will of him who sent me" (Jn. 6:38). Volition is part of the image of God and of the mind of Christ.

Much contemporary psychology (as well as some theology, when we examine its presuppositions) denies the possibility of true volition. People behave in certain ways, but the belief that this behavior springs from conscious choice is an illusion. Begin with a purely empirical presupposition, and this is the only conclusion you can logically reach. Volition, purpose, intention—all are beyond the scope of scientific investigation and therefore presumed not to be real.

By contrast, a Christian begins with the fact of the revealed Word of God. Biblical Christians assume a personal, volitional, conscious God rather than the blindered view of an empirical presupposition. The Christian faith is unthinkable without the fact of the will of God—and, derivatively, the will of man and woman.

The mind of Christ does not turn a Christian into a Spirit-controlled robot. Our goal is not to be "controlled" by the Spirit. Rather, through the presence of the Spirit Christians are enabled to freely exercise their wills to do God's will. Nowhere does Scripture say we are to be *controlled* by the Spirit; rather we are to be *led* by the Spirit, manifesting the fruit of self-control (Gal. 5:22).[15] Christians, of all people, should be "willful," but with their will bowed before God, as creature before the Creator.

The church should give due emphasis to this fact of volition, especially when society either manipulates or preempts human will. In the information age we either find our range of significant choices increasingly limited or else we confront overchoice, a dizzying explosion of choices that tends to numb us.[16] One can choose, for instance, between dozens of insignificant options on a car—colors, styles, accessories, horsepower and so on—but so far not between a gasoline and an electric engine, a far more significant choice.

Equally important is the whole area of advertising and propaganda. John Kenneth Galbraith wrote of the "massive growth in the apparatus of persuasion and exhortation that is associated with the sale of goods." The average person (better known as "consumer") is the target of incessant propaganda about how to use his or her money. "On no other matter, religious, political, or moral, is [one] so elaborately instructed," observed Galbraith.[17]

But politics is not far behind industry. Recent U.S. presidential campaigns have witnessed propaganda efforts unprecedented in extent, expense and sophistication. Computers identify those sectors of the electorate most open to persuasion so that unnecessary effort and expense will not be wasted on unresponsive groups. Similar techniques will likely be repeated in the future with increasing effectiveness and subtlety.

This vast network of persuasion, involving industry, government, education and perhaps even religion, is one of the features of high-tech society. The trend is toward both the limitation and manipulation of significant choices.

What does this mean for Christians? The church faces an increasingly difficult task in imitating the mind of Christ. It will be tempted to rely on secular propaganda techniques to win converts and produce "Christian" behavior rather than taking the harder but deeper road of true spiritual growth-toward-maturity through the recovery of the biblical meaning of the church.

Implications for Church Structure

What does all this mean for wineskins? How should the church be structured so that its members may resist the pulls and pressures of society? How can we have the mind of Christ?

The church must be structured so as to affirm the uniqueness and value of human personality. It must insist that what is true of each person is equally true of the church: It has value because it is the work of God. Many today would reduce the church to a technique, a means to an end, saying that the church exists not for itself but to serve. This is true, but only a half-truth. The church is the Body of Christ. Christ died for the church and loves it, and therefore the church has unique worth. Regardless of what it does in the world, the church has value and meaning because God created it. This is really another way of saying, after all, that salvation is "by grace, through faith," and "not by works." And yet the church is "created in Christ Jesus for good works," which should be its "way of life" (Eph. 2:10).

More specifically, we may identify the following implications for church structure:

Church structure must recognize and honor every person if the mind of Christ is to become a reality in the church. The whole sphere of the personal must be the special domain of the church.

This may sound strange, since Western Christianity has often been rightly criticized for over-emphasizing the individual. But the biblical corrective is not to ride a pendulum swing to the other extreme. Neither is it to seek a bland, middle-of-the-road approach. Rather, the solution is to affirm the breadth of the revealed Word of God: The gospel has both communal and individual dimensions, and both must be incarnated in the church. So any unbiblical swing away from distinct personhood must be resisted.

Look at Jesus Christ, whose mind is to be in us. His life showed solidarity with all humankind. He died for all. But his uniqueness as an individual person stands out clearly, not solely because he was the unique incarnation of the invisible God but because of the very individuality of his humanness. Jesus was not the incarnation of some generalized humanity; he was and is a particular person.

Church structure must be compatible with this personal emphasis. Structures should bring people face-to-face with Jesus Christ as responsible persons. Education and training must focus on the person and not allow anyone to be lost in the group, even while using group dynamics and interaction. In every area of the church's life there must be a recognition that Christ calls, saves and inhabits specific persons for his glory, and that his work will show itself in ways as varied as crystals of snow or leaves on a tree—as varied as human personality itself.

Obviously, this need will require a proper accent on one-to-one relationships in the Christian community. This should be not primarily in the traditional sense of pastor-to-member, but in the sense of a whole glorious web of believer-to-believer relationships that become the hidden structure of community. Here again, small groups are necessary to provide opportunity and stimulus for such relationships.

A crucial implication here is the importance of marriage and the family for the church. These are the basic personality-forming institutions God has given us, and they must function hand-in-hand with the church. In a sense, the Christian home is one of the structures of the church. In God's intent, the church is the family of God and the family is the church of God. We must rethink the family on the basis of the biblical understanding of the Body of Christ.

A person in need never got lost in the crowd when Jesus passed by. This is a parable for church structure today.

Second, *church structure must be flexible and varied.* This is the meaning of spontaneity and self-consciousness, discussed above. Church structure should provide a variety of outlets for ministry and for expressing the meaning of faith in Christ. There must be some freedom of choice in discovering and developing a Christian lifestyle (or variety of lifestyles) for our age, but within the authority of Scripture and the context of Christian community.

The life of the Christian community should produce the kinds of changes suggested in the following example:

In the past couple of years I have had fellowship with several brothers who once served with a Christian organization whose goal was world Evangelization. The zeal within this organization had led to a rule that each staff member must witness a certain number of times per week. Reports had to be filed on this by each one. Finally God began to speak to these particular men about what he wanted in their lives. Not long after leaving this organization, one of these men said to me, "It's really great! I'm just beginning to learn to live. I'm discovering what it really means just to be free to be like Christ.". . .

Another of these fellows shared with me one day the exciting discovery that he had made. He had found that he didn't have to go around with secret cravings lurking beneath the surface all the time. He had found that the resurrection life of Jesus was able to lift him above the problem by replacing it with a wholesome love from God for others. He was free![18]

Structure must be flexible. In those areas where no specific pattern has been revealed, changes should be made as circumstances and biblical fidelity warrant. Such areas include time, place and frequency of meetings, organization for specific ministries, and most aspects of church government. Here flexibility, not just tradition, should rule. The very silence of the Bible concerning specific structures should alert us to their subsidiary and culturally bound nature and remind us that constant re-evaluation in the light of the Word of God is necessary if the mind of Christ is going to become a reality.

To do the work of God in the world the church is naturally forced to adopt structural patterns (organizations, institutions and so on) which are appropriate to the surrounding culture (see chapter 13). But such structures are never the essence of the church. They may be revised, adapted, or even dissolved. In recent years considerable sociological research has been done about flexible, short-term or "self destruct" organizational forms. The institutional church could benefit greatly from such studies. Their application might be useful in areas where the church's structure is organizational in nature, including, especially, denominational structures.

Third, *church structure must help sustain a Christian's life in the world.* The church's task is not to keep Christians off the streets but to send them out equipped for kingdom tasks. The Christian community must be structured for such equipping. The more society becomes hostile to Christian values, the more Christians will depend for their very lives on living, supportive structures of community.

Such structures must reinforce the values of personality through small groups and a new emphasis on the family and other one-to-one relationships. This may require forming special-interest cells for Christians called to specific ministries in the world. And certainly it will mean a serious theological involvement with Scripture to determine the shape of Christian responsibility in society.

A final implication arises here: *Church structure must be built upon spiritual gifts.* The gifts of the Spirit are a witness to the diversity of human personality. Paul emphasizes in 1 Corinthians 12-14, Ephesians 4 and elsewhere that the essential function of spiritual gifts is to build Christian community. This is synonymous with incarnating the mind of Christ in the church. Spiritual gifts form one of the basic foundations for a proper understanding of the church.

Christians—and therefore the whole community of faith— experience the mind of Christ only as God-given spiritual gifts are awakened and exercised. No Christian with an atrophied gift will easily come to demonstrate the mind of Christ. Further, the dynamic interaction of gifts within the community is necessary for achieving the mind of Christ corporately. We understand this on the basis of the figure of the body: The ear hears, not because it enjoys hearing, but that the body may function. The hand grasps, not just because it needs the exercise (which it does!), but that the body may act.

An emphasis on spiritual gifts means church structure which is dynamic, interactive and organic. It means conscious resistance to secular organizational models for the church. The structure of the community must be based on biblical models and figures, not on models taken from industry, education or government. In many cases, a proper emphasis on spiritual gifts means a fundamental rethinking of church structure.

A certain tension, even antithesis, must prevail between the church and society. This tension is biblical, in the spirit of John

17:14-16 and similar passages, and will become more pronounced throughout the world in coming decades. The unique value of the mind of Christ will be denied by society in general, and therefore will become pivotal for the church.

But this is no argument for withdrawal from the world, for building monasteries of the spirit. Nor is it to deny that Jesus Christ is Lord of all creation, that he has "disarmed the rulers and authorities and made a public example of them, triumphing over them" (Col. 2:15). God's plan is still "to gather up all things in him, things in heaven and things on earth" (Eph. 1:10). The church shares with Christ the secret that the present battle will be won by Jesus, for the victory was won on the cross. In the face of a godless society Christians have confidence to work in the world, raising signs of the kingdom which, by faith, they see coming.

Incarnating the mind of Christ in the church requires some clear thinking and some rethinking of the basic structural model of the church. What does it really mean, practically, to structure the church organically? I will now deal with this matter, outlining a basic organic model.

The Ecology of the Church

THE FELLOWSHIP OF the Holy Spirit—the people of God—the mind of Christ. These are essential Trinitarian touchstones for an experience of the church that is biblical and cross-culturally relevant. These are the biblical dimensions that point to a dynamic, organic model of the church, the Christian community.

As Body of Christ, the church is a living organism. All the biblical images of the church point to church models that are living, flexible, and cellular, as we have seen. With this key insight, we can proceed to outline a foundational model of church life.

A key question for every organism: What is its *ecology?* How do all the parts fit together and interact with their environment? What is the ecological equilibrium that sustains a healthy church as it experiences the *koinonia* of the Spirit, incarnates the mind of Christ, and fulfills its Kingdom mission in the world as the people of God?[1]

The church's life may be viewed ecologically as a dynamic interplay of many parts. Like every organism, its health depends on the proper balance and functioning of the parts. Understanding the ecology of the church means discerning the key elements and how these relate to each other.

Paul paints an ecological picture of the church in 1 Corinthians 12, using the analogy of the human body. Each believer is a member of the body, and the health of the whole depends on the proper functioning and interplay of all the members. Paul is in fact thinking ecologically when he says, "The body is a unit, though it is made up of many parts; and though all its parts are many, they form one body. So it is with Christ" (1 Cor 12:12 NIV).[2]

Paul speaks similarly but from a slightly different angle in Ephesians 4:1-16. This is also a picture of church ecology, but the accent is not so much on individual members and gifts as on the dynamic of growing up into Christ and living from the fullness of his grace. The emphasis is on the dependence of the body on the head, Jesus Christ. Yet this picture is also highly ecological: "Speaking the truth in love, we will in all things grow up into him who is the Head, that is, Christ. From him the whole body, joined and held together by every supporting ligament, grows and builds itself up in love, as each part does its work" (Eph 4:15-16).

These passages underscore the fact that the church is a living, charismatic organism dependent on the grace of God. Examining Ephesians and other New Testament passages, we may construct an ecological model that identifies the basic elements of the church's life and shows how these relate to each other.

The following model is a synthesis of the New Testament teachings on the ecology of the church. I emphasize that this is a model. That is, it is not a complete description of the church's life, nor is it the only valid way to view the local church. It is a fairly comprehensive model, however, and it is consistent with Scripture and particularly apt for church life in today's world.

The Purpose of the Church

The model begins with the church's purpose. It is easier to understand the ecology of the church when we know why it exists in the first place.

This starting point really determines everything else. Just as a saw does not serve well as a hammer or a finger as an ear, so the church is powerless when it functions contrary to God's plan. The church has tremendous force when its purpose and functions match God's design. Too often, however, we expect the wrong things from the church—in part because we are not clear about its purpose.

The church is to be sign, symbol and forerunner of the Kingdom of God. The church exists for the Kingdom. More simply, the purpose of the church is to glorify God. So an ecological model orients church life toward God's glory. Using a circle to represent the Christian community, our model then begins to take form as pictured in figure 1.

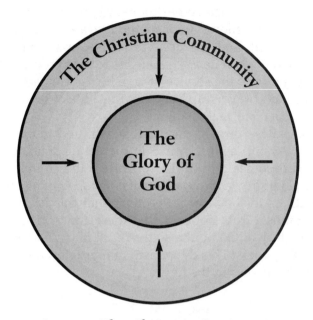

Figure 1. The Christian Community

Functions of the Church

A faithful church glorifies God in many ways. In order to avoid the pitfall of justifying anything and everything the church does simply by saying it is "done for the glory of God," however, we need to identify the most basic functions of the church. What are the essential components of the church's life?

In portraying the church as God's household (*oikos* in the Greek New Testament), it is helpful to view the church as a fellowship of *worship, community* and *witness.* Given the proper biblical and practical rhythm of worship, community and witness, the church maintains a spiritual ecological balance that keeps it lively and faithful. This provides the dynamism and health that allow it to be used dramatically in God's larger plan of redemption.

We find the New Testament church living a life of worship, community and witness. These functions are indicated to some extent by the New Testament words *leitourgia* ("service" or "worship," from which comes the English word "liturgy"), *koinonia* ("fellowship" or "sharing"), and *martyria* ("witness" or

119

"testimony," from which comes the word "martyr").[3] The church is a community or fellowship of shared life, a *koinonia*. The church witnesses to what God has done in Jesus Christ and in its own experience, even when its *martyria* leads to martyrdom. Above all, the church performs the service of worship *(leitourgia)* to God, not just through acts of worship but by living a life of praise to God— the church as a continual doxology.

Drawing these three elements together, and giving a certain priority to worship as the church in the act of praising God, the model then becomes that of figure 2. Here the church is seen as glorifying God through its worship, its life together in community, and its witness in the world. Recalling that this is an ecological model, we must stress not only that these functions are directed toward the glory of God but also that each one interacts with and influences the others. This dynamism of interrelationships is highlighted by the arrows in the figure.

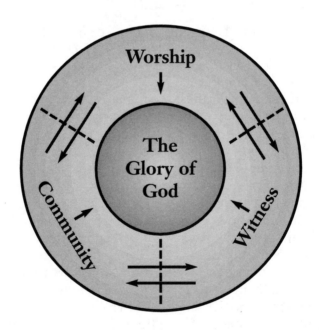

Figure 2. Worship, Community, and Witness

These functions stand out clearly in the early days of the Christian church. In Acts 2:42 we read that the first Christians "devoted themselves to the apostles' teaching and to the fellowship, to the breaking of bread and to prayer." Further, we read that they shared their goods and homes with each other so that no one had need and all had a house fellowship in which to worship God and be strengthened for witness in the world.

1. *Worship.* The early Christians "devoted themselves . . . to the breaking of bread and to prayer." This describes the church at worship. Bread-breaking probably means the early Christian *agape* meal in which believers celebrated the Lord's Supper in their house fellowships. Meeting together in their homes as well as in large-group worship, first-century Christians kept their church life vital through frequent praise and prayer.

Acts 4:22-31 pictures the church at worship. Peter and John had been arrested and then released by the Sanhedrin. The believers came together to praise God and to pray for boldness. And God answered. "After they prayed, the place where they were meeting was shaken. And they were all filled with the Holy Spirit and spoke the word of God boldly" (Acts 4:31).

Paul tells the Ephesians: "Speak to one another with psalms, hymns and spiritual songs. Sing and make music in your heart to the Lord, always giving thanks to God the Father for everything, in the name of our Lord Jesus Christ, [submitting] to one another out of reverence for Christ" (Eph 5:19-21). We are to "teach and admonish one another with all wisdom," singing "psalms, hymns and spiritual songs with gratitude to God" (Col. 3:16).

Worship—praising God and hearing him speak through the Word—is the heart of being God's people. In the Old Testament we read of the great festivals of the children of Israel. These, as well as the whole sacrificial system, focused on worshipping God.

Down through history, in every land and language, worship has been the central activity of the church, its very life blood. This is appropriate, for worship is, above all, the church praising God. In worship the church celebrates who God is and all God has done for his people. It renews its covenant to live for his glory. Worship comes first among all the things the church does, for its special concern is the glory of Almighty God.

Worship means more, however, than worship *services*. We are to live a *life* of worship. Everything we do is to glorify God. This life of worship comes to special focus and intensity, however, in the regular weekly worship celebration of God's people.

Each week is a journey through time. The journey brings us face to face with the values, pressures and seductions of an idolatrous age. Getting through the week means turning a deaf ear to countless advertisements for clothes, cars, magazines, entertainment centers and other items, even while we listen for the cries of human need. Unless we plan otherwise, the week will be programmed for us by job or school commitments, errands, TV schedules, our acquaintances and many other demands. The world closes in on us.

This is why Paul says in Romans 12, "Don't let the world around you squeeze you into its own mold" (Phillips). Rather we are to offer ourselves as living sacrifices to God. This is genuine worship (Rom 12:1-2).

Worship is the opening in an enclosed world. The world tries to make us like itself. It draws a circle around us, blocking out the higher, brighter world of the Spirit. We are not to deny the present world nor to flee from it. Rather we are to learn how to live like Jesus within society. We are to be lights in the world (Mt. 5:14-16; Phil. 2:15).

Here is the key. In worship the curtains of time and space are thrown back, and we see anew the realm of the Spirit. Worshipping God in spirit and truth gives us a window on eternity. It changes our lives as we see again that we really do live in two worlds. We begin to see from God's perspective: "I entered the sanctuary of God; then I understood" (Ps. 73:17).

Certainly as Christians we worship God privately in our own times of prayer and devotion. But worship is especially the business of the church gathered. Alone in prayer, we tend to focus on our own needs, problems and hurts. There is nothing wrong with this, provided private prayer is balanced by corporate praise. God made us to glorify him *together*. We are to be a worshipping, praising community. There is something about being together, blending our hearts and voices together in praise, that lifts us away from our own concerns and focuses our eyes on Almighty God. And then something strange happens: In looking at God himself, we find our own lives turned around, healed and prepared for service in the world. The more clearly we see Jesus, the more we see him pointing "outside the gate" (Heb. 13:13), into the world.

This is what worship can and should do for us. But the ways we benefit from worship are, in fact, secondary. The great concern is God himself. We worship God, not to feel better nor even to be more "spiritual," but because he commands and invites us to worship him. In our praise to God, we worship the King.

2. *Community.* The first Christians devoted themselves to "the fellowship" (Acts 2:42). As sharers in God's grace, they gave themselves to being and becoming the *community* of God's people. In Acts and throughout the New Testament we see building Christian community or fellowship as a basic function of the church. The believers "broke bread in their homes and ate together with glad and sincere hearts, praising God and enjoying the favor of all the people" (Acts 2:46-47). This is a basic way of glorifying God.

God makes us a community and wants us to grow continually as a fellowship of believers, being "built up until we all reach unity in the faith and in the knowledge of the Son of God and become mature, attaining to the whole measure of the fullness of Christ" (Eph 4:12-13).

This is edification in the New Testament sense. It is *oikodomein,* building up the household *(oikos)* or community of faith. As W. A. Visser't Hooft has noted, "In the New Testament edification is not used in the subjective sense of intensification and nurture of personal piety. It means the action of the Holy Spirit by which he creates the people of God and gives shape to its life."[4] Biblically, edification is community-building with the person and character of Jesus as the goal.

In the biblical ecology of the church, community is as important as worship. Just as a household is not really a family if it doesn't meet and spend time together, so believers don't really experience the church without Christian community. They do not really "discern the Body" (see 1 Cor. 11:29). Just as the human body cannot live without its vital organs, so the church cannot thrive without community.

Biblically, community means shared life based on our new being in Jesus Christ. To be born again is to be born into God's family and community. While forms and styles of community vary, any group of believers that fails to experience intimate life together has missed the real meaning of Christ's Body. To be the

Christian community means to take seriously that believers are members of each other, and therefore to take responsibility for the welfare of Christian brothers and sisters in their social, material and spiritual needs.

3. *Witness.* In the life of the church, worship and community spark the church's witness.

This was so in Acts. The praise and fellowship described in Acts 2:42-47 brought an interesting result: "The Lord added to their number daily those who were being saved" (Acts 2:47). Later when the Jerusalem church was persecuted and many believers fled to other areas, "those who had been scattered preached the word wherever they went" (Acts 8:4). Jesus told his followers before his ascension, "You will be my witnesses in Jerusalem, and in all Judea and Samaria, and to the ends of the earth" (Acts 1:8). The book of Acts is the history of the church's witness throughout the Roman world in response to Jesus' words.

A church weak in worship has little will for witness. Nor does it have much to witness about. Similarly, a church with no vital community life has little witness because believers are not growing to maturity and learning to function as healthy disciples. Where community is weak, witness is often further compromised by an exaggerated individualism. Witness may degenerate into inviting people to God without involving them in Christian community.

In a healthy congregation, witness springs not only from Jesus' specific commission (Mt. 28:19-20; Acts 1:8) but also from the impulse of Pentecost and the dynamic of Christian community life. These are the primary springs of the church's will to witness in the world. A living Christian community has both the inclination and the power to witness. It witnesses both from concern for human need and for the sake of the coming Kingdom of God. In God's economy, the church's witness has Kingdom significance.

Viewed ecologically, witness is not the primary purpose of the church but the inevitable and necessary fruit of a worshipping, nurturing community. Thus it is a high priority of the church's life in the world.

Exploring the Model

The basic elements of worship, community and witness may be expanded to clarify how they in fact function. Just as these parts combine to shape the life of the church, so each in turn depends on the health of its component parts.

Worship, community and witness may be analyzed in several ways. One way, which seems to possess a certain natural logic and balance, is to view worship as the interplay of *instruction, repentance* and *celebration;* community as consisting of *discipline, sanctification* and *the gifts of the Spirit;* and witness as a combination of *evangelism, service* and *justice.* Figure 3 depicts this fuller ecology of the church.[5]

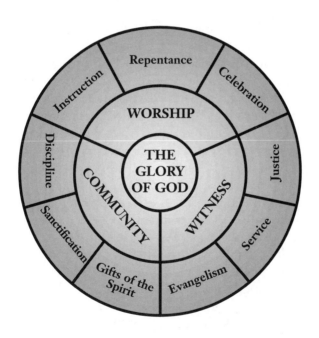

Figure 3. The Ecology of Church Life

Let us see how each of these aspects functions in the church's life.

Celebration is the church in the act of praising God. In worship the church celebrates God's person and works through music, liturgy, spontaneous praise and other means.

The Christian life is a life of celebration. The word *celebrate,* like the word *worship,* suggests honoring someone else. In worship we celebrate God's worth. But because of who God is and what he has done, celebration means joy as well. Christians are a joyous, singing people because they know the secret of who God is. Their joy comes from the freedom God gives from the bondage and hopelessness of sin.

Giving praise to God for who he is touches the deepest fibers of our being. Praise reaches down even below the conscious levels of our personalities because deep within us God has made us for himself. As we praise God, the deep wells of soul and spirit are stirred. This is why worship not only glorifies God but also frees, cleanses and strengthens us.

The church at worship celebrates a God of action, not abstraction. Worship is celebrating God's acts in history and especially in Jesus Christ. This is realism, not mysticism. It includes celebrating God's work in our lives and our life together in the Christian community. Coming together as sisters and brothers in Christ, we share the mystery and secret not only of sins forgiven but also of fellowship given. So we "rejoice with those who rejoice; mourn with those who mourn" (Rom. 12:15).

Special joy comes to believers in celebrating the coming new age, the manifestation of the fullness of God's reign. *Worship liberates the church for the Kingdom.* We praise God not only for what he has done but for what he will do. Already in faith we anticipate and celebrate the day when we will sing, "The kingdom of the world has become the kingdom of our Lord and of his Christ" (Rev 11:15). In worship we celebrate God's economy (*oikonomia*) and Kingdom—now and for the future. The church celebrates the future present, knowing that "the kingdom of God is not a matter of eating and drinking, but of righteousness, peace and joy in the Holy Spirit" (Rom 14:17). This kind of worship I call "reality therapy" because it denies the reality of a materialist, three-dimensional worldview and celebrates *the truth* about God, our lives, and where history is going.

The Lord's Supper is a key part of this great celebration. The Eucharist recalls God's work in Christ and signals forth both the reality of the church and the promise of the Kingdom. The church is in fact a sacramental community.[6]

Instruction as part of worship involves the church in hearing God's voice through the Word read, taught or otherwise spoken. In worship the movements of celebration and instruction are movements of the Spirit and the Word.

The church is the community of the Word as much as it is the community of the Spirit. It is the environment where we learn from God. Not only do we speak to God in worship; even more importantly, we listen to God speaking to us. We worship in the Spirit as we receive the Word. This is a basic part of worship. God has revealed himself through his Word. We can be his faithful people only as we hear, understand and obey it.

The community of God's people lives by the Word applied to our hearts by the Spirit. Paul gives us a picture of God's Word in the life of the church when he says, "Let the word of Christ dwell in you richly as you teach and admonish one another with all wisdom, and as you sing psalms, hymns and spiritual songs with gratitude in your hearts to God" (Col. 3:16). Thus Paul reminds us that sharing the word in worship is something believers do with one another, not something for a person to do alone. The passage suggests also that instruction often merges into celebration.

Public worship should be built around the Word of God. Often worship begins with a verse of a psalm or other Scripture calling us to worship, uniting our focus on God himself. This reminds us of our primary vocation to glorify him.

We often hear God's Word also in Scripture lessons from the Old and New Testaments. The regular use of Scripture in worship teaches us the ways of God with his people—all that he has done in the past and all he intends for the present and the future.

Scripture can be used profitably and creatively in a variety of ways in worship. Readings can he tied to the main events of the Christian year. For many centuries the church has patterned its yearly worship around the events of Jesus' life. The Christian year begins not with New Year's Day but with Advent, the announcement of Christ's coming, four weeks before Christmas.

Then follow the seasons of Christmas, Epiphany (the public appearing and ministry of Jesus), Lent (centering on Jesus' suffering and death), Easter, and Pentecost.

Pentecost, celebrating the coming of the Holy Spirit and the life of the church, begins the longest season of the year (about six months), bringing us round again to Advent. Pentecost is a good period to recall also how God has worked down through history and right up to the present, using Scriptures that recount God's mighty acts. Following the Christian year keeps our attention on God's acts through Christ rather than allowing us to slip into a rhythm dominated by secular holidays and commercial seasons.[7]

Besides the normal reading, reciting or singing of the Word, the Scriptures can be presented in drama, responsive or antiphonal reading, dance and other ways. Just as the psalms tell us to use poetry and music in worship, so they also speak of liturgical dance.

Many of the psalms are suited to dramatic or responsive reading. Psalm 107, for instance, tells the story of God's faithfulness to his people through history. The refrain recurs: "Let them give thanks to the LORD for his unfailing love and his wonderful deeds" for his people. Dividing the psalm into sections according to these refrains, a group of readers (or the whole congregation, divided into sections) can read the entire psalm, raising a rising chorus to God for his unfailing faithfulness.

Our church once did something similar with the book of Revelation. To introduce a sermon series on Revelation that would begin the next week, we structured a whole worship celebration around the book. Different people read major sections, interspersed with joyful singing and other elements of worship. It was an unforgettable service. The Revelation of Jesus Christ came alive as we exalted the King of Kings and Lord of Lords and celebrated, by faith, the final outcome of history.

Particularly important in worship is the public proclamation of the Word through teaching and preaching (1 Tim. 4:13; 5:17). God has chosen through the "foolishness" of preaching "to save those who believe" (1 Cor 1:21). Preaching means both public proclamation of the Word to unbelievers and teaching the Word to believers as part of regular worship. While God enables all Christians to read and understand the Word on their own, he also gives special gifts for preaching and teaching (1 Cor. 12:28; Eph 4:11; Acts 6:2). The church should seek to identify and encourage members who have these gifts and should pay special attention to the words of those so gifted, even while it continues to "test everything," holding on to the good (1 Thess. 5:21), through private study and small-group gatherings.

Repentance is perhaps seldom seen as part of worship, but it really fits into the rhythm of Word and response. To celebrate God while our lives contradict the gospel and we remain unrepentant is false worship. Yet this is true of much of the church in North America and elsewhere. God broke into the sacred worship of unrepentant Israel to say, "I hate, I despise your religious feasts; I cannot bear your assemblies. . . . Away with the noise of your songs! I will not listen to the music of your harps. But let justice roll on like a river, righteousness like a never-failing stream!" (Amos 5:21, 23-24). Worship is closely linked with God's Kingdom and justice in the ecology of the church, and therefore with repentance.

At several points in its history, Israel truly heard God's Word, repented and was renewed. It could then truly celebrate the Lord's goodness. When Isaiah saw the Lord "high and exalted," he repented of his uncleanness and was thus prepared to serve God effectively (Is. 6:1-10). The proclamation of the Kingdom in the New Testament begins with a call to repentance (Mt. 3:2). And James says to the church, "Wash your hands, you sinners, and purify your hearts, you double-minded. Grieve, mourn and wail. Change your laughter to mourning and your joy to gloom. Humble yourselves before the Lord, and he will lift you up" (Jas. 4:8-9).

God's word to the church is often "Repent!" (Rev 2:22), not "trust" or "believe." When the church is unfaithful to God, worship without repentance is blasphemy. It will bring judgment, not blessing.

One of the rhythms of worship, then, is the rhythm of instruction, repentance and celebration. In these acts we celebrate not only God's acts in the past, but also his mercy in renewing us, forgiving us, and accepting us as his people.

Practically, this means we should provide for repentance as well as praise in our worship. Often repentance is part of the church's liturgy, as in the General Confession in the *Book of*

Common Prayer or the ritual of Holy Communion. This is most appropriate and reminds the church of the need for repentance. But repentance needs to be made specific, both in the personal lives of believers and in the corporate life of the Christian community.

As the economy of God and the priorities of his Kingdom become clearer to the church, repentance will increasingly be seen as a key to Kingdom faithfulness. Repentance from self-centeredness, gluttony and oppression, and from trusting the false gods of wealth, nationalism, political ideology and military power can open the doors to renewal and to a new identification with Earth's poor and suffering. In this sense, repentance can be a key to radical renewal. In North America it is not so much the nation that needs to repent as it is the church, which claims to be serving God and his Kingdom but often is really serving itself or the subtle deities of technology and security.

Discipline, Sanctification and Spiritual Gifts

The church's life together in community requires as much attention as does worship. This is the real meaning of "the fellowship of the Holy Spirit," as we saw in chapter 7. *Vital worship depends largely on how much care is given to nurturing the church's shared life.* We may think of this aspect of church ecology as including *discipline, sanctification* and *spiritual gifts.*

Discipline means discipleship, building a community of people who are truly Jesus' disciples. The church is not a social club or a chance catch of people; it is a community of believers called and "membered" together by the grace of God. The church is a covenant people. In fidelity to God as revealed in Scripture and in Jesus Christ, Christians accept responsibility for each other and agree to exercise discipline as needed in order to keep faith with God's covenant. In this way the church takes seriously the many scriptural injunctions to warn, rebuke, exhort, encourage, build up and disciple one another in love.

Jesus said in Matthew 18:20, "Where two or three come together in my name, there am I with them"—surely one of the most amazing statements in Scripture. This verse comes, however, at the end of a section where Jesus speaks of sins and conflicts and the need to confront one another. So Jesus is speaking about more than merely *being with* him. He is speaking about what it means to be a community of disciples. To be "together with Jesus" for a short while is no problem. But when we start living our lives together as Christian brothers and sisters, helping each other to be faithful to our calling as Christians, problems arise. Sins crop up. We offend each other, get on each other's nerves. And so confrontation, discipline and reconciliation become necessary. This, too, is part of what it means to "be with Jesus." Part of the ecology of the church is learning how to live and function together as a community of discipline.

We don't naturally follow the Jesus way. We tend to stray, doing our own thing instead of God's thing. We need someone to guide us, to encourage us, to praise us when we do well and correct us when we do wrong. We need discipline—both the internal discipline that flows from centering our lives in Christ and walking in the Spirit, and the external discipline that comes from being accountable to and for one another.

God has saved us and made us responsible for each other. This is why Paul says, "Each of you should look not only to your own interests, but also to the interests of others" (Phil 2:4). Believers must be ready to take some agreed responsibility for their own lives and for the lives of their sisters and brothers in the faith.

This is one of the reasons small-group structures are essential in the church. The New Testament shows a level of Christian life that is distinct from the world and that simply fails to happen without some form of small-group structure. Hebrews 3:13 says we should "encourage one another *daily*, . . . so that none . . . may be hardened by sin's deceitfulness." This requires frequent intimate gatherings, for without such constant mutual support we will likely be deceived by sin.

Hebrews 10:25 is related: "Let us not give up meeting together, as some are in the habit of doing, but let us encourage one another." These passages seem to suggest frequent gatherings for encouraging one another. They point to times of meeting in smaller groups for nurture and discipline, as well as other frequent contacts among believers. This is a key issue of structure, to which we will return in a later chapter.

A number of Scriptures speak of the need to encourage, exhort and even rebuke one another in the church—James 5:16, 1 Thessalonians 5:11, Colossians 3:16, Romans 12:15, for example, and the passage from Matthew 18 already mentioned. These passages picture a level of Christian commitment and behavior that requires some form of small covenant-cell to sustain. These qualities are simply lost to the church when it does not meet with sufficient frequency, intimacy and commitment to permit them to develop.

Sanctification is closely related to discipline and to the edification *(oikodome)* of the church, discussed earlier. Sanctification is the Spirit's work restoring the image of God in believers and in the believing community. It is having the mind of Christ, producing the fruit of the Spirit. It is the manifestation of Christ's character in his Body.

This is the work of the Holy Spirit in believers and in the Christian community. Jesus wants to make us like himself. Part of the purpose of life together is the sanctification of believers. God wants a holy people—a people distinct from the world in order to be engaged with the world. This holiness is not to be molded after some abstract or otherworldly notion of saintliness, but according to the character of Jesus Christ.

Personal piety has a place in God's household. The disciplines of devotion and growth in grace are legitimate concerns for those who are determined to put God first in their lives. Yet the church always runs the danger of turning this focus into spiritual narcissism or subjectivism. Other aspects in the total ecology of the church, if kept in balance, can effectively counter this tendency. As Richard Foster suggests in *Celebration of Discipline,* the inward life and disciplines must be balanced by the outward and corporate life and disciplines.[8] Bible study, devotional reading, prayer and fasting, and other means toward a holy life are important disciplines in themselves. They become potent in Christian experience when they are part of the larger balanced ecology of the Christian community.

Christians should be those who are concerned, as John Wesley often said, with "all inward and outward holiness." Our personal habits, stewardship of our bodies, and commitment to honesty, integrity and purity are as important for the health of the church as is our more outward witness in the world. Both are part of the sanctified life.

Sanctification is, above all, the ministry of the Holy Spirit. We are saved "through the sanctifying work of the Spirit and through belief in the truth" (2 Thess. 2:13). God continues his sanctifying work in us and in his body as we allow his Spirit to cleanse, fill and liberate us. "Where the Spirit of the Lord is, there is freedom. And we, who with unveiled faces all reflect the Lord's glory, are being transformed into his likeness with ever-increasing glory, which comes from the Lord, who is the Spirit" (2 Cor. 3:17-18).

This freedom flowers when the church functions according to God's ecology and economy. It does not happen otherwise, or at least not to the extent God intends. For sanctification is part of the larger picture of the church's life.

The priority of sanctification is another reason why the church needs close-knit small groups or covenant cells to undergird its life. Such groups are just as important as the other aids toward spirituality and edification which the church provides.

Spiritual gifts are a particularly important part of the community life of the church. We will look more closely at spiritual gifts in the next chapter, but here we must note their place in the essential ecology of church life.

The gifts of the Spirit become vital and practical when they are awakened, identified and exercised in the context of shared Christian community. In God's ecology, the fruit of the Spirit and the gifts of the Spirit go together. To stress one over the other is to distort God's plan for the church, crippling the body.

Spiritual gifts are not "things" that God gives, like presents or bonuses. Rather they are *manifestations of his grace* in the church. They are God's grace working through the personalities of believers, preparing and enabling them for their particular ministries, so that the church may be edified, the Kingdom of God may be established, and God may be glorified in all. The key biblical passage for understanding gifts ecologically is Ephesians 4:11-16.

Spiritual gifts are one of the foundation stones of the ministry of God's people. Gifts are awakened, identified and channeled as believers are intimately tied in to the community life of the church. Further, as the range of gifts is awakened and begins to function, these gifts quicken other aspects of the church's life and mission. Thus gifts are one of the most important links in the church's ecology. The functioning of gifts provides much of the dynamism of the church's witness and worship, as well as building community. If we trust God and his working in the body, we will find that the Spirit raises up people with the necessary gifts to make the full ecology of the church function. This, then, becomes key to the church's witness in the world.

In sum, we may say that discipline, sanctification and spiritual gifts constitute the ecology of the church's community life. The purpose of their functioning together is to build the household of God so that it can indeed live "to the praise of his glorious grace" (Eph. 1:6).

Evangelism, Service and Justice

The key elements in the church's witness are *evangelism, service* and *justice*. Adding these elements, we get a fairly complete picture of the total ecology of the church.

Historically, the church has found it difficult to hold evangelism, service and the prophetic witness of God's justice together. But where the church's evangelistic witness has been buttressed by loving service in the spirit of Jesus and an authentic concern for justice, the church has been at its best and has made its greatest impact for the Kingdom.

Evangelism—sharing the good news of Jesus and the Kingdom—is always important in a biblically faithful church. In a healthy church evangelism usually just happens. Little is said about it. This is probably why the New Testament gives many examples of the church's evangelistic witness but says little about the need to evangelize. Today, however, we must stress evangelism in the church's ecology because church history and accumulated tradition show the tendency either to exaggerate or neglect the missionary thrust of the gospel.

Ecologically, evangelism strongly affects the other areas of the church's life. A church which is not evangelizing becomes ingrown and self-centered. With time, it often turns legalistic through the weight of tradition, the lack of new blood and the loss of the vitality that new converts bring. Evangelistic fruitfulness enlivens both the church's worship and its community life. The church was made to grow and reproduce itself. Where this does not happen, its vitality suffers. New converts in a church fellowship are like the birth of a baby into a family.

Service means the church's servant role in the world, following the example of Christ. Like evangelism, service is part of the overflow of the life of the Spirit in the church. It is rooted in the church's community life because Christian service means both serving one another in the household of faith and reaching out in service to the world. Service is grounded also in worship, for in worship we are reminded of what God has done for us. His Word calls us to follow Jesus to the poor, the suffering and the oppressed.

Justice is also an essential part of the church's witness to the world. Jesus commissioned us to make God's "kingdom and righteousness" or justice our first priority (Mt. 6:33).[9] In the biblical ecology, evangelism and service combine with the church's prophetic justice witness, renewing society and genuinely pointing ahead to the Kingdom.

The church that incarnates this tripartite biblical ecology is prophetic in the world—prophetic both by what it is and what it does. It is prophetic when it creates and sustains a reconciled and reconciling community of believers, recognizes and identifies the true enemy, renounces the world's definition and practice of power, and works for justice in society.[10] Most of all, the church is prophetic when by its worship, community and witness it points toward and manifests the new age of the Kingdom.

The church is God's prophetic word and witness in the world when it stands with and for the poor. Jesus made it plain that this is where he intends us to stand, as we have seen (Mt. 25:31-46). When we serve the poor, we are not taking Christ to them; we're merely going where he already is and making him known (Mt. 25:40). Thus the church's evangelism and service themselves become prophetic, showing God's concern with justice for the oppressed. Standing with the poor is both a pointer to the new age and a condemnation of the powers of the present age (whether political, economic, physical or spiritual) that are content with providing security for the rich and advice for the poor. This is another way of saying the church must be a visible sign of the Kingdom.

From the ecological viewpoint, then, evangelism, service and justice combine and interact to constitute the church's witness in the world. And this witness is nourished and authenticated (or else starved and betrayed) by the quality of the church's worship and community life.

Using the Model

This ecological model for church life can be strategically useful. In addition to aiding our understanding, it is helpful in diagnosing the condition of a church and in solving the question of structure.

Problems in a church frequently trace to an imbalance in the ecology of worship, community and witness. Viewing the church as a living organism helps us discern the sickness, the pathology, that may need correcting so that the fellowship can have a balanced and healthy life. The need, therefore, is to diagnose the problem and correct it.

When the church is weak in *worship*, its life becomes humanistic and subjective. The impulse for evangelism is often lost. When *community* life is anemic, believers remain spiritual babes, failing to thrive in Christ. Worship may become cold and formal, and witness weak or overly individualistic and programmed. If the church's *witness* is the problem, the fellowship may become ingrown and self-centered. The church drifts into legalism in order to guard its life, and has little growth or impact. Investigating these various areas can be very revealing to a church that is seeking to be free for the Kingdom but senses something is wrong.

Renewal, then, means bringing the church to the level of normal health that God intends. Actually the goal is not *renewal* so much as it is *vitality*. Renewal should be understood as building a vital fellowship which works together with God's Kingdom purposes.

This model can be used also to explore questions of church structure. If worship, community and witness are basic for church health, then the question arises whether the church really has functional structures in these areas. Some of the components of church life may require more structure than others. But if the various elements presumed in the model are all essential, then we must ask whether the church is *structured for life* in these areas. Structure won't bring life, but its absence can bring death. A family can live without a house, but it will be healthier if it has shelter. Structure is the skeleton which gives shape to life.

In raising the question of structure, we must remember that the church is primarily a charismatic organism rather than an institution or organization. Therefore structures created for the church's life must fit a organic model. They must be charismatic in the sense of being grounded in God's grace *(charis)* and the Spirit's gifts *(charismata)*. Structures ought not to be a mishmash of programs and organizations that clash with the essential nature of the church itself.

These are the dimensions and some of the dynamics of the ecology of the Body of Christ. Forming functional, faithful wineskins in today's world means finding practical ways to help the church experience the balanced ecology of worship, community, and witness.

The Place of Spiritual Gifts

GOD CREATES. HENCE man and woman, created in the divine image, also create. The Spirit of God who was "moving over the face of the waters" at the dawn of creation is the same Spirit who, according to Scripture, operates in the church, giving to each Christian "the manifestation of the Spirit for the common good" (1 Cor. 12:7).

The Christian faith makes room for gifts and creativity on the basis of the important biblical doctrine of the gifts of the Spirit. Yet, many Christians are confused about spiritual gifts and unaware of the creativity they imply. Too often our Christian traditions—implicitly, if not explicitly—deny the possibility of real creativity. The institutional church often shows a serious and crippling misunderstanding of the biblical concept of giftedness. Even though interest in spiritual gifts has grown considerably in recent decades, this interest has often generated more heat than light.

One cannot really understand what the New Testament means when it speaks of the church unless one understands what it teaches about the gifts of the Spirit. Gifts are part of the essential ecology of the church as a spiritual organism, as we have seen. They are primarily a matter not of *individual* Christian experience but of the body life of the church. Gifts are given for, and in the context of, community.

I have already suggested in chapter 6 how our misunderstanding of spiritual gifts affects our concept of the pastoral ministry and feeds the "Superstar" idea, and in the last two chapters we noted that structure must be compatible with gifts. We need now to discuss somewhat more thoroughly the place of spiritual gifts in the life of the church.

The church in its institutional form often makes little room for spontaneous spiritual gifts. Worse, it does not need spiritual gifts in order to function more or less successfully. When the local church is structured after an institutional rather than a charismatic model, spiritual gifts are replaced by aptitude, education and technique, and thus become superfluous.

Several common misunderstandings of spiritual gifts today need to be corrected and shown for what they are: unbiblical tendencies that effectively quench the working of the Holy Spirit in the Christian community. I suggest, in particular, five such tendencies.

1. *The tendency to deny or discredit spiritual gifts.* In its most extreme form, this tendency says the gifts of the Spirit were given as miraculous signs at Pentecost but have no legitimacy today. Gifts of healing, prophecy and tongues are no longer considered valid. In a milder form this tendency admits, in theory, the validity of spiritual gifts but in practice is suspicious of them and tends to discredit them. All spiritual gifts, and especially the more controversial ones, are thought to be superfluous at best and heretical at worst.

Such a position, however, rashly limits the operation of the Holy Spirit and the applicability of the New Testament to our day. There is no more warrant, for instance, for applying chapters 12 and 14 of 1 Corinthians exclusively to the early church than there is for limiting the thirteenth chapter in this way. Gifts and love go together—in the twentieth century as in the first.

The denial of spiritual gifts really indicates a basic misunderstanding of the nature of such gifts—and, in fact, of the church. Those who fear spiritual gifts (and often the problem is, really, one of fear) usually conceive of such gifts as highly individualistic, irrational and eccentric manifestations that disturb the unity of the Body of Christ. But such a caricature is not at all what the Bible means by the gifts of the Spirit.

Spiritual gifts cannot be discounted without a corresponding devaluation of the biblical understanding of the church and the Spirit-filled life. The *charismata* are not something artificially tacked on; neither are they temporally or culturally bound. They are cross-culturally valid, and it is their presence in the church which makes the church cross-culturally relevant. It is no accident that Paul, both in Romans 12 and Ephesians 4, relates the unity of the Spirit's ministry in the church to the diversity of gifts. The appeal to "present your bodies as a living sacrifice" and "be transformed by the renewal of your mind" is followed by the appeal, "Having gifts that differ according to the grace given us, let us use them" (Rom. 12:1-6). Both injunctions are for today.

Incidentally, none of the New Testament discussions on gifts restrict any specific gift to men or women only. Apparently the New Testament church welcomed whatever gifts God gave, regardless of whether the recipient was a man or a woman.

We simply have no authority to declare specific gifts invalid. It may be difficult to accept the full range of biblical teaching here, but this is necessary to avoid impoverishing the church. And it is absolutely essential for a truly biblical doctrine of the church and its ministry.

2. *The tendency to over-individualize spiritual gifts.* Western Christianity in general has tended to over-individualize the gospel to the detriment of its communal and collective aspects.[1] Contemporary conceptions of spiritual gifts have suffered from this tendency. Thus spiritual gifts are too often thought of as strictly a matter of a believer's "private" relationship to God, without regard for the Christian community. In contrast to this, Paul repeatedly emphasizes that the Spirit's gifts are for the edification of the church and lose their significance if this emphasis is lost. The general principle is, "To each is given the manifestation of the Spirit *for the common good*" (1 Cor. 12:7). Each gift graciously given is balanced by community responsibility and interaction. Paul prefaces his comments on gifts in Romans 12 with the words, "We, though many, are one body in Christ, and individually members one of another" (Rom. 12:5). This is the biblical balance, and spiritual gifts can rightly be understood only in this context.

According to the New Testament, the community of believers acts as the controlling context for the exercise of gifts, thus discouraging individualistic aberrations. And gifts must operate in this way. The church is, to use Gordon Cosby's phrase, "a gift-evoking, gift-bearing community." When the church really functions in this way, the various gifts not only reinforce each other, they also act as check-and-balance to prevent extremes. Here the New Testament analogy of the body is helpful. The hand or foot is prevented from some extreme action by its connection to the body's various organs and systems. Functioning as part of the body, the hand is helpful and nearly indispensable, but cut off it becomes grotesque and useless. So it is with spiritual gifts.

Here, incidentally, small Bible study groups are especially useful. The small Spirit-led group builds community and provides the context for both awakening gifts and disciplining their use. Through many such cells, the whole larger community of the church is edified.

Spiritual gifts are given not merely for personal enjoyment or even primarily for one's own spiritual growth, although this, too, is important. Gifts are given for the common good, "that the church may be edified" (1 Cor. 14:5).

3. *The tendency to confuse spiritual gifts and native abilities.* The error here lies in the drift to one extreme or the other: to make spiritual gifts and native abilities either synonymous or else opposites.

Each person is born with latent potentialities which should be developed and employed to the glory of God. This is stewardship. But when the New Testament speaks of spiritual gifts, it goes beyond this. Paul says the Holy Spirit "apportions to each one individually as he wills" (1 Cor. 12:11). This suggests a direct, immediate relationship between God and the believer through conversion and life in the Spirit. The gifts of the Spirit result from the operation of the Spirit in the life of a believer, and so are something more than merely the wise and faithful use of native abilities. Gifts must be understood as, literally, *gifts* of the *Spirit*.

But how and when does the Spirit operate? Only after conversion? The Holy Spirit is the Spirit of creation that was "moving over the face of the waters," the same Spirit who said to Jeremiah, "Before I formed you in the womb I knew you, and before you were born I consecrated you; I appointed you a prophet to the nations" (Jer. 1:5). God is sovereign and omniscient, and we must not suppose that he begins to work in a person's life only after conversion. There really is no such thing as a "native" ability, after all. "What have you that you did not receive?" (1 Cor. 4:7). It is not too much to say that God in his foreknowledge has given to each person at birth those talents that he later wills to awaken and ignite. A spiritual gift is often a God-given ability that has caught fire.

A native capacity does not really become a gift of the Spirit until it is given over to the Spirit and used by him. The principle of crucifixion and resurrection, of dying and rising, applies. Natural abilities remain in the plane of powerless human works until given to God in self-sacrifice.

In his perceptive discussion of spiritual gifts in *Full Circle*, David Mains writes,

> *In those areas where I have natural abilities, such as a facility for public speaking, the difference between their being talents or gifts of the Holy Spirit is found in my attitude. If I recognize the talent as from God, and in prayer and continual dedication commit it to Him to be used in ministry in a special way, it becomes a gift of the Holy Spirit with supernatural expression. The proof of this is seen in the gradual way God increases the gift for His service.*[2]

So talents and gifts are neither synonymous nor polar opposites. Both, after all, are bestowed by God. It is no accident that converted salesmen often make good evangelists. God is not capricious. Although we must not limit the sovereign working of the Spirit, yet we may normally expect some correspondence between a person's native abilities and personality traits—latent or developed—and the spiritual gifts God will bring forth. The Spirit intends to transform us into what we were meant to become, not into Xerox copies of each other.

4. *The tendency to exaggerate some gifts and dismiss others.* This is one of the most serious and most common distortions of spiritual gifts: the tendency to restrict legitimate gifts to only those we are familiar or comfortable with. How serious this aberration has become is seen in the fact that discussions of spiritual gifts often get sidetracked on the question of tongues. The tendency to think of spiritual gifts only in terms of the more spectacular gifts such as tongues, healing or prophecy is an aberration which must be avoided. All gifts are important, all gifts are necessary, and all are given by God for the common good.

An examination of the relevant biblical passages suggests that the various gifts mentioned are intended as representative, not exhaustive. The multiform operation of the Spirit may awaken an infinity of gifts. Gifts may be as varied as human personality. The

New Testament lists the specific leadership gifts of apostle, prophet, evangelist and pastor-teacher (Eph. 4:11; 1 Cor. 12:28). But such designations as utterance of knowledge, helps, service, acts of mercy and so forth, may be understood as general categories which include a wide spectrum of specific gifts and ministries.

Thus any ability ignited and used by the Holy Spirit—whether in music, art, writing, intercessory prayer, homemaking, hospitality, listening or whatever—is a legitimate spiritual gift. If God has given the gift, then it is good and is intended to be used. The biblical teaching is plain: "As each has received a gift, employ it for one another, as good stewards of God's varied grace, . . . in order that in everything God may be glorified through Jesus Christ" (1 Pet. 4:10-11).

The problem, too often, is the failure to affirm the full range of gifts—the failure to appreciate "God's varied grace." The fact is that all gifts are important, and none is an anomaly when exercised rightly in the context of community. Thus it is as wrong to over-emphasize preaching and teaching and to deny tongues and healing as it is, on the contrary, so to stress the more spectacular gifts that the more mundane gifts are lost sight of. The Holy Spirit acts so "that there may be no discord in the body" only when all gifts are affirmed and operate cooperatively. To quote David Mains again,

> *Every true member of the local church has a minimum of one gift, and most people have many. Since no one has every gift, and everyone has at least one, there exists an interdependence among the members of the church. Scripture teaches (1 Cor. 12:22-25) that the less spectacular gifts are more necessary than the showy ones. In other words, the church can go a long time without a miracle, but let it try to exist without acts of mercy or contributions! . . . How disabled the body of Christ has become because our primary purpose for church attendance has been to hear one man exercise his gifts, rather than to prepare all the people to develop their gifts for ministry, not only within the church but also to society.*[3]

A healthy church will expect, identify and awaken the varied gifts that sleep within Body. When all gifts are affirmed under the leadership of the Holy Spirit and in the context of mutual love, each gift is important and no gift becomes an aberration. Whether the Holy Spirit chooses to grant to a particular local congregation all the gifts mentioned in Scripture remains, of course, a divine option. It's not up to us. We have nothing to say about it, for The Holy Spirit is sovereign. We can be sure, however, that God will give to each local church all the gifts really necessary for its own growth in love and ministry.

5. *The tendency to divorce spiritual gifts from the cross.* This tendency arises from the failure to incarnate the tension between the cross and the *charismata,* between Passover and Pentecost. It is the tendency, on the one hand, to stress gifts in such a way that the cross is lost sight of and the community is fractured by self-centeredness. Or just the opposite: to deny any emphasis on gifts for fear of self-centeredness and spiritual pride.

What is the biblical view? How can the fact of all believers discovering and exercising their gifts be reconciled with Christ's fundamental words, "If any want to become my followers, let them deny themselves and take up their cross and follow me" (Mk. 8:34 NRSV)?

There *is* a danger here, for spiritual gifts are often misunderstood. The New Testament teaching is not a call for each Christian to "do his or her own thing" and forget the welfare of the group and the need of the world. Ministry is not determined exclusively by personal desire, but by the cross.

And yet, biblically, there is no contradiction between gift-affirmation and self-denial. In fact, the two go together. The biblical principle, again, is that of death and resurrection. As each of us is crucified with Christ and dies to our own will, the Holy Spirit resurrects within us our particular significant gift. So the spiritual gift, rightly exercised, is not self-centeredness. It is self-giving.

But we must go further even than this. *We discover the true meaning of crucifixion as we really begin to exercise our gifts.* Faithful ministry of the gifts of the Spirit will lead us into depths of self-giving we never imagined—and God planned it that way. This is the way we are created, psychologically, emotionally and spiritually.

So we come face to face with the life and death of Jesus Christ, God's Son and the perfect human. We may suppose that Jesus possessed, at least potentially, all the gifts of the Spirit. He publicly exercised many of them—apostle, evangelist, healer, prophet, teacher, helper, comforter, friend. The faithful exercise of his ministry led him not to the throne, but to the cross. But it led beyond as well—to resurrection.

"For to this you have been called, because Christ also suffered for you, leaving you an example, that you should follow in his steps" (1 Pet. 2:21). *Here* we find the meaning of the gifts of the Spirit.

Elizabeth O'Connor wrote insightfully along this line in her book, *Eighth Day of Creation.* "When one really becomes practical about gifts, they spell out responsibility and sacrifice," she says, Further,

> *The identifying of gifts brings to the fore . . . the issue of commitment. Somehow if I name my gift and it is confirmed, I cannot "hang loose" in the same way. I would much rather be committed to God in the abstract than be committed to him at the point of my gifts. . . . Doors will close on a million lovely possibilities. I will become a painter or a doctor only if denial becomes a part of my picture of reality. Commitment at the point of my gifts means that I must give up being a straddler. Somewhere in the deeps of me I know this. Life will not be the smorgasbord I have made it, sampling and tasting here and there. My commitment will give me an identity.*[4]

Spiritual gifts come to their full biblical legitimacy and meaning only in the rhythm of incarnation-crucifixion-resurrection.

Much of the church is still confused today about spiritual gifts. And yet the biblical teaching is clear, if we seek it. The various distinctions suggested here are attempts to peel away layers of culturally defined conceptions so that the biblical teachings can shine through.

The urgent need today is that spiritual gifts be seen and understood in the context of ecclesiology, as in the New Testament. A biblical understanding of spiritual gifts is absolutely essential for a biblical conception of the church. For this will determine whether our ecclesiology is based on a charismatic or an institutional model.

When spiritual gifts are misunderstood—through being over-individualized, denied, divorced from community or otherwise distorted—the church suffers. The church truly becomes the church only when the biblical meaning of spiritual gifts is recovered. A church whose life and ministry is not built upon the exercise of spiritual gifts is, biblically, a contradiction in terms.

In recent decades the Holy Spirit himself has seemingly been calling his church back to the reality of spiritual gifts. Local churches have been renewed, books have been written and a gradual gift-consciousness has developed.

Many churches today are discovering the practical meaning of spiritual gifts, as is increasingly obvious in writing on church renewal. From the perspective of missions and missionary strategy, many missiologists now stress the importance of discovering and using spiritual gifts in the church's worldwide mission.[5]

No teaching is more practical than solid instruction about the gifts of the Spirit. The discovery of one's spiritual gift often turns a frustrated, guilt-ridden Christian into a happy and effective disciple. In my own case, the discovery of gifts clarified the ministry to which God has called me and opened new vistas and opportunities of service. When I identified and named my gifts, it seemed as if all the contradictory pieces of my life fell into place. I found the key to what God was doing in and through my life.

Happy, effective service should be the result of identifying and coming to terms with the gifts the Spirit has given us. For it is Christ himself who "gives gifts" to men and women in order that they may happily glorify him.

The Small Group as Basic Structure

A SMALL GROUP of eight to twelve people meeting informally in homes is the most effective structure for the communication of the gospel in today's high-tech society. Such groups are better suited to the mission of the church in an urban world than are traditional church services, institutional church programs or the mass communication media. Methodologically speaking, the small group offers the best hope for the discovery and use of spiritual gifts and for renewal in church and society.

This is one of the principal conclusions that arises from the analysis of the previous chapters. I argue for the small group as basic church structure not primarily because its usefulness has been abundantly demonstrated in recent years through the proliferation of neighborhood Bible studies, cell churches, 12-step groups, and various kinds of sharing and *koinonia* groups—though this is highly significant. My argument springs, rather, from the inherent character of small groups and their essential compatibility with the biblical ecology of the church.

The small group was the basic unit of the church's life during its first two centuries. There were no church buildings then; Christians met almost exclusively in private homes. In fact, the use of small groups of one kind or another seems to be a common element in all significant movements of the Holy Spirit throughout church history. Early Pietism was nurtured by the *collegia pietatis*, or house meetings for prayer, Bible study and discussion. The small group was a basic aspect of the Wesleyan Revival in England, with the proliferation of John Wesley's "class meetings."[1] Small groups undergirded the Holiness Revival that swept

America in the late 1800s and led, in part, to the modern Pentecostal movement.[2] More significantly, the road to the Reformation was paved by small-group Bible studies.[3] If nothing more, these facts surely suggest that small groups are conducive to the reviving ministry of the Holy Spirit.

Today the church needs to rediscover what the early Christians found: Small group meetings are essential to Christian experience and growth. The success of a church function is not measured by body count. Without the small group the church in a high-tech society simply does not experience one of the most basic essentials of the gospel—true, rich, deep Christian soul-fellowship, or *koinonia*.

Advantages of Small Group Structure

The small group offers several advantages over other forms of the church:

1. *It is flexible.* Because the group is small, it can easily change its procedure or functions to meet changing situations or to accomplish different objectives. Being informal, it has little need for rigid patterns of operation. It is free to be flexible as to the place, time, frequency and length of meetings. It can easily disband when it has fulfilled its purpose without upsetting the institutional seismograph. These things can be said of virtually no other aspect of most church programming.

2. *It is mobile.* A small group may meet in a home, office, shop or nearly any other place. It is not bound to that building on the corner of First and Elm that we call "church." It can go where the people are (or where the action is) and does not have to rely on persuading strangers to enter a foreign environment.

3. *It is inclusive.* A small group can demonstrate a winsome openness to people of all kinds. As Elton Trueblood says, when people are "drawn into a little circle, devoted to prayer and to deep sharing of spiritual resources," they discover they are welcome for their own sake, "since the small group has no budget, no officers concerned with the success of their administration, and nothing to promote."[4]

True, small groups can become exclusive. But true *koinonia* grounded in Bible study, worship, and prayer guards against this. More basically, integration into the total ecology of church life described in chapter 10 guards against exclusiveness and "koinonitus." Functioning in this way, the small group provides a context where a person can be seen, as Oswald Chambers put it, "as a fact, not as an illustration of a prejudice." Thus it holds some hope for overcoming social and racial barriers.

4. *It is personal.* Christian communication suffers from impersonality. Often it is too slick, too professional, and therefore too impersonal. But in a small group person meets person; communication takes place at the personal level. This is why, contradictory as it may seem, small groups may actually reach more people than the mass communication media. The mass media reach millions superficially but few profoundly. The church should use all available forms of communication, but in proclaiming a personal Christ nothing can substitute for personal communication.

5. *It can grow by division.* A small group is effective only while small, but it can easily reproduce itself. It can multiply like living cells into two, four, eight or more, depending on the leadership and vitality of each group. Endless possibilities for numerical growth without correspondingly large financial outlays or spiritual-impact dilution is one of the amazing qualities of healthy groups.

6. *The small group can be an effective means of evangelism.* The evangelism which will be most effective in a high-tech world will use small groups as its basic methodology. It will find that the small group provides the best environment in which sinners can hear the convicting, winning voice of the Holy Spirit and come alive spiritually through faith. It will find that faith is contagious when fellowship is genuine. Robert Raines testifies in *New Life in the Church,* "I have watched proportionately more lives genuinely converted in and through small group meetings for prayer, Bible study, and the sharing of life than in the usual organizations and activities . . . of the institutional church."[5]

7. *The small group requires a minimum of professional leadership.* Many church members who could never direct a choir, preach a sermon, lead a youth group or do house-to-house visitation can lead a small group. Competent leadership is needed in such groups, but experience has shown that good leaders can be developed in the average church through one to two key initial groups and some ongoing discipling. A staff of trained professionals is not needed.

8. *It is adaptable to the institutional church.* The small group does not require throwing out the organized church. Small groups can be introduced without bypassing or undercutting the church. The serious incorporation of home fellowships and cell groups into the overall ministry of the church does require some adjustment, however, and is bound eventually to raise questions about priorities. The small group is best seen as an essential component of the church's structure and ministry (its basic ecology), not as a replacement for the church.

Jess Moody says, "We will win the world when we realize that fellowship, not evangelism, must be our primary emphasis. When we demonstrate the Big Miracle of Love, it won't be necessary for us to go out—they will come in."[6] I would say rather, our emphasis should be evangelism through fellowship, and especially through *koinonia*. This is coupling love's miracle with Christ's invitation.

It is questionable whether the institutional church can have a significant evangelistic ministry today through traditional methods. It may be able to build a denomination or megachurch and carry out programs, but it will never turn the world rightside up.

Most of today's methods are too big, too slow, too organized, too inflexible, too expensive and too professional ever to be truly dynamic in a fast-paced high-tech society. If the contemporary church would shake loose from plant and program, from institutionalism and inflexibility, and would return to the dynamic of the early church, it must seriously and self-consciously build its ministry around the small group as basic structure.

The Place of the Small Group in Church Structure

Today many Christians take some form of small group for granted, whether or not they really understand its biblical and theological grounding. For me personally, it was Scripture and reading on church renewal that first led me to this conviction. Three books which were especially helpful, and which remain prophetic, are Lawrence O. Richards' *A New Face for the Church* and George W. Webber's *God's Colony in Man's World* and *The Congregation in Mission.*[7]

George Webber was one of the first persons in the post-World War II era to see the small group as basic to church structure, as more than just a technique or program. Out of several years' experience in the early days of the East Harlem Protestant Parish in New York City, Webber convincingly presented the case for the small group as the basic unit in the life of the congregation. His analysis is especially relevant because it grows out of experience in an inner-city setting—in a sense, a laboratory for the future.

Webber's insights and experiences are worth examining a little more closely. He wrote,

A new structure of congregational life is called for which makes provision for genuine meeting between persons, a context in which the masks of self-deception and distrust will be maintained only with difficulty and in which men and women will begin to relate to each other at the level of their true humanity in Christ.[8]

Thus each church should "make basic provision for its members to meet in small groups, not as a side light or an option for those who like it, but as a normative part of its life."[9]

Why? In part because of today's patterns of living. In small-town America, and even in urban America in the past, Christians often lived close together in stable communities. But urbanization and technology have changed these patterns, not only in America but in many parts of the globe. Modern technopolis is a different world. Thanks in part to urban mobility, we live in several distinct worlds in the course of a week: office, shop, neighborhood, school, club, and now, cyberspace. The church is only one world among many for the majority of Christians. Thus today "we do not live in natural, human communities where we know each other in Christ and where, during the week, we have a chance to consider the implications of our faith together. *This must be built into the very structure of the life of the congregation.*"[10]

True, the church often brings believers together at other times than Sunday—but usually only the pious few, and then not in a way that encourages *koinonia*. The average church has no *normative structure* for true sharing and fellowship.

The small group, then, must be both supplemental and normative—supplemental in that it does not replace large-group worship; normative in the sense of being basic church structure, equally important with the larger worship celebration.

Webber thus pictures a necessary dual focus for the local congregation. We must maintain the old focus of corporate worship but also insist on the new focus of the small group: "We must participate in the common worship life of the congregation, and we must also participate in a group within that life of the whole congregation in which we seek to understand the meaning of our commitment to Jesus Christ and the implications for our life as colonists in the world."[11]

According to Acts 2:46 the early Christians spent their time attending the temple together and breaking bread in their homes. "These are the two foci of our life as Christians about which I am speaking," says Webber. "We join in congregational worship. We meet in small groups."[12] Thus the small group is not optional; it is essential structure. Notes Webber,

> *Experience in many places suggests that such meetings must be both normative for a congregation and regular. The moment they become the possession of a pious few they are likely to lose momentum. This is not to suggest that a majority of the congregation will necessarily participate, but it does mean that the expected pattern for the congregation, shared in by the responsible leadership, does focus on small groups. The important point is that the small unit be seen, not as a temporary expedient or special form, but as an essential structure of congregational life in our day.*[13]

Groups Exist for Service

But merely *having* small groups is not enough. Their function must be clearly understood. Their purpose is objective, not merely subjective. If the focus is only on personal spiritual growth the groups turn inward and become self-defeating—like regularly pulling up a plant by the roots to see if it is growing. Rather, the purpose of such groups "must be defined in objective terms that involve work to be done and goals to be achieved."[14] They exist for service; they are "enabling groups," equipping disciples for Christ-like obedience in the world.

For the purpose of obedience and service, the small groups set before themselves the objective task of Bible study. Here's the key: Something happens in Bible study in a small group that does not happen elsewhere. The Holy Spirit gives the unique gift of *koinonia* which makes Bible study come alive. Thus Webber discovered, "People who have listened politely to sermons for years, when they gather together to listen to God's word from the Bible, are most likely to squirm in the face of honest confrontation, and only with difficulty can they brush aside the demands upon their lives."[15]

This awakening may not happen immediately, however. Webber as well as others have noted that weeks or months may pass before miracles happen. Says Robert Coleman, "The members must be honest with God and with each other. It may take awhile to come to this freedom and trust. After all, you are not prone to bare your soul to people you do not know."[16] Partly for this reason the small group must be essential church structure, not merely a tentative experiment. *Koinonia* is not to be experimented with, but to be experienced.

The Small Group and Church Institutionalism

One of the most promising aspects of the small group is just this point of its possibilities as a structure. The small group offers some hope of a way through the suffocating institutionalism of much church life. The average local church is weighed down with excess organizational baggage that at the same time seems unavoidable. What to do? How does one find a pattern for congregational life which is "functional for mission"?

In a passage of great significance for a relevant and biblical ecclesiology, Webber writes,

> *The clear demand of mission is that the multiplicity of congregational organizations be eliminated. A missionary congregation does not need a women's missionary society, but women engaged in mission. For male fellowship let the men join the Rotary or the union and in that context become salt that preserves the secular structures of community. . . . The small groups in a congregation, along with the vestry, session, or governing board, can manage to fulfill the necessary institutional requirements of the congregation without setting up a host of organizations to fill out in full a denominational table of organization for the local church. . . .*
>
> *Thus we conclude that congregational organization must be functional for mission. The time in small groups must have one*

> *eye always on the worldly involvements of their members, so that*
> *the precious time the church requires will be used for equipping*
> *the saints.*[17]

For illustration, Webber mentions the annual every-member canvass that had been used to underwrite the church budget. Usually this involved considerable time and organization. But several inner-city churches have conducted the canvass through existing Bible study groups that already reached into most parish homes—a system remarkably similar to that of the early Methodist "class meetings" in England. The objective was reached at considerable savings of time and effort. Says Webber, "It sounds simple and is simple."[18]

The small group can become basic structure in a local church if there is the vision for it and the will to innovate. The change cannot come, however, without rethinking traditional programs and structures. The midweek prayer meeting may have to go in favor of a number of midweek small-group meetings so that the small groups do not take up another precious weeknight or become something merely tacked on. Other traditional services and activities may be replaced by small group meetings. In fact, the whole organization of the church's life will require review.

The small group is not a panacea. No human effort can bring the church to greater faithfulness in meeting the needs and problems of its day except as the Holy Spirit directs and fills. But the small group is an essential component of the church's structure and life. In order for men and women to be moved by the Holy Spirit they must be open to God and to others—and this openness develops best in a context of the supporting love and fellowship of other sincere seekers after God.

In the early days of the great Methodist Revival in England some 250 years ago, John Wesley discovered the importance of the small group for his day. He set up a network of small cell groups—"class meetings"—for the growth of sincere seekers. He soon saw surprising results. In reply to criticism he wrote, "Many now happily experienced that Christian fellowship of which they had not so much as an idea before. They began to 'bear one another's burdens,' and 'naturally' to 'care for each other.' As they had daily a more intimate acquaintance with, so they had a more endeared affection for each other."[19] In short, the early Methodists discovered the *koinonia* of the Holy Spirit through the use of small groups. The wineskins were useful for the wine. Nothing was more typical of the Methodist Revival than a dozen or so persons meeting together in private homes.

The Bible does not prescribe any particular pattern of church organization. But today's practical necessities suggest the need for small groups as basic church structure—as always when the church has been at its best.

Church Structure in Space and Time

Church and Culture

THE BIBLE PAINTS a distinct profile of what the church is intended to be and gives the early history of the church in two cultural contexts: Palestinian Jewish society and first-century Graeco-Roman society. On the basis of this biblical witness, the church in each epoch faces the task of forming those wineskins most compatible with its nature and mission within its particular culture.

But here we face a prickly problem. We see that biblically the church is the people of God and the fellowship of the Holy Spirit, not an organizational institution. But when we look at the contemporary church, we see not only (or even primarily) the church as people; we find also a proliferation of denominations, institutions, agencies, associations and buildings to which the name "church" is applied. The Bible does not speak of such institutions and structures. They clearly have no explicit biblical basis. How do we handle these structures in light of the biblical picture of the church?

We face here the problem of *culture.* Both organizational patterns and architecture are expressions of particular cultural values and norms. How can we, in a practical way, maintain a biblical understanding of the church while the church embodies itself in such a vast array of diverse, culturally-colored wineskins?

Drawing on the emphases of the previous chapters, I would like now to relate the biblical view of the church and church structure to the problem of culture.[1]

Donald McGavran wrote of "the magnificent and intricate mosaic" of humankind represented by the world's cultures and emphasizes that "adaptation of Christianity to the culture of each piece of the mosaic is crucially important." The goal of the church is "to multiply, in every piece of the magnificent mosaic, truly Christian churches which fit that piece, are closely adapted to *its* culture, and recognized by *its* non-Christians as 'our kind of show.'"[2]

This is happening today in a remarkable way. The Body of Christ is amazingly and gloriously diverse, and increasingly so as the gospel fire leaps cultural walls and ignites people who have never heard. As this happens, however, the question of culture becomes crucial for the church. How does one deal with the problem of wineskins in a situation of increasing cultural diversity?

Traditional Views of the Church

It is common to speak of the *visible church* and the *invisible church*. While this distinction is not wholly satisfactory, it does help resolve a persistent problem: the painful contrast between what the church is called to be (the holy, righteous people of God) and what it too often in fact is (an unholy, cantankerous human organization). Making the visible-invisible distinction at least allows us to say there *really is* a holy, spiritual, God-directed church that transcends what the eye normally sees.

The biblical view of the church may be contrasted with two traditional views which correspond roughly to the visible church/invisible church distinction.[3] These are the *institutional view* and the *mystical view*.

The institutional view identifies the visible institutional structure with the essence of the church, making no significant distinction between the two. Thus most denominations are called churches, and in practice *church* and *denomination* mean the same thing.

Although this view reached its most elaborate form in Roman Catholicism, it is also common among Protestants. In Protestantism, however, it does not represent so much a theoretical or theological position as it does common, popular usage. On reflection, many would doubtless say the institution is not the same thing as the church, and the idea of the invisible church would be brought in. But in fact popular usage does not make this distinction, and *church* is equated with the organizational structure.

There may be nothing wrong with calling denominations or institutional structures churches—but this is not what the Bible means by *church!* When Paul or Peter or Jesus Christ say *church,* they clearly do not refer to an institution or organization. That is not what *visible church* would have meant to the apostles.[4]

In contrast, the mystical view puts the church far above space, time and sin as an ethereal reality comprising all true believers in Christ and known only to God. It is therefore invisible, in the sense that its precise limits are unknown to anyone on earth. The mystical view attempts to solve the problem of the embarrassing disparity between the institutional, or visible, church and the church as biblically described. It is a little like Plato's theory of ideas: What we see may be imperfect, but a perfect church exists invisibly.

There is, of course, an invisible church—or rather we should say, the true church of Christ surpasses visible reality. But this also is not what the Bible normally means by *church.* While the Bible does speak of the great multitude of the saved from every nation and every age who comprise the one true church, this is not the common meaning of *church* in the New Testament. Nor is the biblical meaning highly mystical. There may be an invisible church, but such an immaterial conception is not very helpful in understanding the life and growth of the church on earth and in history. When the Bible says *church,* it does not normally mean an invisible, ethereal reality divorced from space and time any more than it means an institutional organization.

Both these views have one thing in common: They fail to take culture seriously. In the institutional view the church becomes so wedded to and embedded in its particular culture that the culturally determined nature of much of its life and structure is overlooked. Thus the church becomes culture-bound. This creates problems especially when cultures change or when cross-cultural witness is attempted.

In the mystical view, however, the church floats nebulously above culture and never gets tangled in the limiting dimensions of space, time and history. Cultural factors, which affect theology, structures and mission, are not taken into account.

Thus both the institutional view and the mystical view are inadequate. Both cloud the clear biblical meaning of the church— one by too close an identification of the church with culture, the other by removing the church from culture. In both cases it is really culture which becomes "invisible."

To understand the church biblically we must move beyond the traditional visible-invisible model and move back to the prior and more fundamental biblical view. We must take the church seriously in such a way that space, time and history (the dimensions of culture) are also taken seriously.

How the Bible Sees the Church

In contrast to traditional views, the Bible pictures the church in the midst of culture, struggling to maintain its fidelity while tainted by the corrosive oils of paganism and religious legalism. This view is sharply relevant today.

Let us briefly examine three essential aspects of the biblical view.

1. *The Bible sees the church in cosmic-historical perspective.* Scripture places the church at the very center of God's cosmic purpose. This is seen most clearly in Paul's writings, and particularly in the book of Ephesians. Paul was concerned to speak of the church as the result of, and within the context of the plan of God for the whole creation (Eph. 1:9-10, 20-23, 3:10, 6:12).[5]

What is this cosmic plan? The first three chapters of Ephesians state it clearly: That God may glorify himself by uniting all things in Christ through the church. The key idea is *reconciliation*—not only the reconciliation of man and woman to God, but the reconciliation of all things, "things in heaven and things on earth" (Eph. 1:10). Central to this plan is the reconciliation of people to God through the blood of Jesus Christ. But the reconciliation Christ brings extends to all the alienations that result from human sin: within oneself, between persons, and between humans and their physical environment. Mind-boggling as the thought is, Scripture teaches that this reconciliation even includes the redemption of the physical universe from the effects of sin as everything is brought under proper headship in Jesus Christ.[6]

Paul emphasizes the fact of *individual* and *corporate* salvation through Christ, then goes on to place personal salvation in cosmic perspective. The redemption of persons is the *center* of God's plan, but it is not the *circumference* of that plan. Paul alternates between a close-up and a long-distant view, for the most part focusing on the close-up of personal redemption, but periodically switching to a long-distance, wide-angle lens that takes in "all things"—things visible and invisible; things past, present and future; things in heaven and things on earth; all the principalities and powers—the whole cosmic-historical scene.[7]

Historically, the people of God have disagreed not so much over *what* God is doing in the world but over *when* he will do it. Most Christians admit that, one way or another, God is bringing history to a cosmic climax. But one branch has said, "Not now; *then!*" And, the other has said, "Not then; *now!*" Those who postpone any real presence of the kingdom until after Christ's return ("Not now; *then*") do not expect any substantial renewal now except in the realm of individual human experience—not in politics, art, education, culture in general, and not even, really, in the church. The other side so emphasizes present renewal in society in general that both personal conversion and the space-time future return of Christ are denied or eclipsed, and the depths of human sinfulness are not taken seriously.[8]

Hopefully, Christians today throughout the world are coming to see that the kingdom of God is neither entirely present nor entirely future. The kingdom of God (the uniting of all things in Jesus Christ) *is now here*, is *coming*, and *will come*. Francis Schaeffer well expressed this biblical balance when he spoke of a "substantial healing" now in all the areas of sin-caused alienation. Christians are not to put all real reconciliation off into an eschatological future; neither are they to expect total perfection now. What God promises is a substantial healing now and a total healing after Christ's return.[9] Putting this fact in terms of God's cosmic plan, we may say that God has *already begun* the reconciliation of all things in human history.

What, then, is the role of the church in God's cosmic plan? According to Ephesians 3:10, God's will is that "through the church the wisdom of God in its rich variety might now be made known to the rulers and authorities in the heavenly places." The church is the earthly agent of the cosmic reconciliation God wills. God is bringing about his cosmic purpose through the instrumentality of the church. This means the church's mission is broader than evangelism. Evangelism is at the center of the church's role as agent of reconciliation, and therefore is the first priority of the church's witness in the world. But the mission of the church extends to reconciliation in other areas as well.

German missiologist Peter Beyerhaus clarifies the church's role in God's cosmic purpose when he says the church is "the new messianic community of the kingdom." Says Beyerhaus, "The messianic kingdom presupposes a messianic community." Thus the church in the world "is the transitory communal form" of the kingdom of God "in the present age, and through his church Christ exercises a most important ministry towards the visible coming of the kingdom." So the church is God's earthly agent of his coming reign. Beyerhaus defines this kingdom as "God's redeeming lordship successively winning such liberating power over [people's] hearts, that their lives and thereby finally the whole creation (Rom. 8:21) become transformed into childlike harmony with his divine will."[10]

This is the cosmic perspective in which the Bible sees the church. The kingdom of God is coming, and to the extent this coming takes place in space-time history before the return of Christ, it is to be accomplished through the people of God.

2. *The Bible sees the church in charismatic rather than institutional terms.* According to the New Testament, the church is a charismatic organism, not an institutional organization. The church is the result of the grace (Greek, *charis*) of God. It is through grace that the church is saved (Eph. 2:8) and through the exercise of spiritual gifts of grace *(charismata)* that the church is edified (Rom. 12:6-8; Eph. 4:7-16; 1 Pet. 4:10-11). Thus the church is, by definition, *charismatic*. As Clark Pinnock observes, "According to Scripture, the Church *is* a charismatic community."[11]

The church's essential characteristic is life, as suggested by biblical figures for the church. Its life is an organized life, to be sure. But much of this organization is secondary and derivative. It is the result of life. The church is, first of all, a spiritual organism with its own organic structure. Only secondarily does it develop organizational expressions.

The New Testament and the writings of the first church fathers show that the early church saw itself as a charismatic community, not as an organization or institution. "Most church historians agree that the apostolic church was a charismatic, spiritual fellowship," says Donald Bloesch.[12] With the gradual institutionalization of the church, however, the idea of the church as an organization became more prominent and largely crowded out the charismatic-organic view, especially in the West, where Roman views of law and the state influenced the church. Thus "in the history of theology the Church as assembled community of the faithful has been too often neglected in favor of the church as institution," notes Roman Catholic theologian Hans Küng.[13]

In the biblical view, God gives his gracious gift of salvation on the basis of Christ's work and through the agency of the Holy Spirit. This provides the basis of the church's community life. The pure light of God's "manifold grace"[14] is then refracted as it shines through the church, producing the varied, many-colored *charismata*. This provides the basis for the church's diversity within unity. The church is edified through the exercise of spiritual gifts as "the whole body, joined and knit together by every ligament with which it is equipped, . . . promotes the body's growth in building itself up in love" (Eph. 4:16).

This is an important key to a healthy, growing church. In order for the church to reach its true biblical potential, it must be based on a charismatic model, not an institutional model. Churches that structure themselves charismatically are largely prepared for the future. But churches which are encased in rigid, bureaucratic, institutional structures may soon find themselves trapped in culturally bound forms which are fast becoming obsolete.

3. *The Bible sees the church as the community of God's people.* The essential biblical figures of Body and Bride of Christ, household, temple or vineyard of God, and so forth, give us the basic idea of the church. But these are metaphors and not definitions. I believe the most biblical definition is to say that the church is the community of God's people.[15] The two key elements here are the church as *a people*, a new race or humanity, and as a *community* or fellowship. We have already discussed these dimensions of the church in chapters 7 and 8.

People and community are two poles which together make up the biblical reality of the church. On the one hand, the church is the people of God. This concept, with rich Old Testament roots, underlines the objective fact of God's acting throughout history to call and prepare "a chosen race, a royal priesthood, a holy nation, God's own people" (1 Pet. 2:9). Here the emphasis is on the *universality* of the church—God's people scattered throughout the world in hundreds of specific denominations, movements and other structures. Seen in cosmic-historical perspective, the church is the people of God.

On the other hand, the church is a community or fellowship, a *koinonia*. This accent, found more in the New Testament, grows directly out of the experience of Pentecost. If peoplehood underlines the continuity of God's plan from Old to New Testament, community calls attention to the "new covenant," the "new wine,"the "new thing" God did in the resurrection of Jesus Christ and the Spirit's baptism at Pentecost. The accent here is on the informality of the church in its intense, interactive community life at the level of the local congregation. Seen as a charismatic organism, the church is the community of the Holy Spirit.

The church, then, is the community of God's people. It is a charismatic organism established by God as the agent of his plan for human history. As such, it is cross-culturally valid and can be implanted and grow in any human a culture.

Church Structure in Cross-Cultural Perspective

If the church is the community of God's people, what shall we say then about the diverse institutions, organizations, denominations and architectural structures commonly included under the umbrella *church*? How do such structures relate to the church as God's community?

The two most common tendencies have been either to say that these structures are actually a part of the essence of the church, and thus "sacralize" them,[16] or else to take an anti-institutional stance and insist that all such structures are invalid and must be abandoned.

A more helpful option, however, is to view all such structures as parachurch structures which exist alongside of and parallel to the community of God's people, but are not themselves the church. These structures are useful to the extent they aid the church in its mission, but are human inventions, culturally determined. Whereas the church itself is part of the new wine of the gospel, all parachurch structures are wineskins—useful, at times indispensable, but also subject to wear and decay. The church is the community of God's people, and this is what the Bible means by church. The church can be nothing other than this! Institutional structures, then, are best seen as something different from the church—potentially useful aids to the church's life and ministry, but never a part of the essence of the church. Wineskins, not the wine.

Normally, "parachurch structures" have been thought of as extra-denominational or interdenominational organizations such as the Billy Graham Evangelistic Association or the National Association of Evangelicals. Denominations themselves are not usually thought of as parachurch structures. But since the church biblically understood is always people and can only be people, therefore any institutional structure, whether a denomination, a mission agency, a Christian college, an evangelical publishing house or an evangelistic association, is a parachurch structure.

In other words, from the biblical standpoint both an evangelistic association and a denominational organization are parachurch structures, while the communities of believers within these structures are the church. Parachurch structures, including denominations, may be legitimate and necessary, but are not the church. This conclusion seems inescapable in the light of biblical teachings about the church's true nature.

Does this mean that all structures are parachurch structures, that no structures are themselves part of the essence of the church? Not necessarily. The church is a body and therefore has an organic body structure and ecology. To be biblically valid, any structures which are truly *church* structures can only be structures which are charismatic and organic. Anything else is a parachurch structure. Institutions and organizations may have their validity as parachurch structures, but should not be confused with the church as the community of God's people.

The Bible itself does, however, give us some principles about the organic structure of the church, and some basic church structures are discernible in the life of the New Testament community. I have already mentioned these in previous chapters, and in a moment I will summarize them.

I want first, however, to point out several benefits that come from distinguishing between the church and parachurch structures: (1) That which is always cross-culturally relevant (the biblically understood church) is distinguishable from that which is culturally bound and determined (parachurch structures). Thus one is free to see the church as *culturally relevant and involved* and yet not as culturally bound. (2) One is free also to modify parachurch structures as culture changes, for these are not themselves the church and therefore are largely culturally rather than biblically determined. (3) Finally, this distinction makes it possible to see *a wide range of legitimacy* in denominational confessions and structures. If church structures are not themselves the church and are culturally determined, then whole volumes of controversy and polemics fall to the ground. Widely varying confessions are freed (at least potentially) to concentrate on what unites them—being the people of God and carrying out their kingdom tasks—while relegating structural differences to the plane of cultural and historical relativity. Thus the crucial consideration for structure becomes not biblical legitimacy but functional relevancy.

Figure 4 suggests further implications of this distinction between the church and parachurch structures.

The Church	*Parachurch Structures*
1. God's creation	1. Human creation
2. Spiritual fact	2. Sociological fact
3. Cross-culturally valid	3. Culturally bound
4. Biblically understood and evaluated	4. Sociologically understood and evaluated
5. Validity determined by spiritual qualities and fidelity to Scripture	5. Validity determined by function in relation to the mission of the church
6. God's agent of evangelism and reconciliation	6. Human agents for evangelism and service
7. Essential	7. Expendable
8. Eternal	8. Temporal and temporary
9. Given by divine revelation	9. Shaped by human tradition
10. Purpose: to glorify God	10. Purpose: to serve the church

Figure 4.
Differences between the Church and Parachurch Structures

Guidelines for Church Structure

From the biblical picture of the church we can now distill four fundamental principles for structure. I believe these principles provide a basic biblical foundation for church structure in any cultural context and help lead to effective witness and growth.

1. *Leadership should be based on the exercise of spiritual gifts.* Hierarchical or organizational patterns must not be permitted to obscure or overwhelm the basic biblical pattern of charismatic (that is, Spirit-appointed and endowed) leadership, open to whomever the Spirit chooses.

In the New Testament, leadership was at first provided by the original eleven apostles, and later by Paul and an expanding group of other apostles, prophets, evangelists, pastors, teachers, bishops, deacons and elders. All these leadership functions relate to spiritual gifts.[17] It is clear therefore that in the New Testament leadership was based on the exercise of spiritual leadership gifts which were recognized (either formally or informally) by the church.[18]

All spiritual gifts should be stressed, not just the leadership gifts. But leadership gifts are especially crucial, for their function biblically is precisely to awaken and prepare the other gifts (Eph. 4:11). Thus not only leadership, but the entire life of the church is based on spiritual gifts—or, more precisely, it is based on Christ who awakens spiritual gifts in each member of the community.

2. *The life and ministry of the church should be built on viable large-group and small-group structures.* The early church's common life of worship, fellowship, nurture and witness reveals a dual emphasis—"in the temple and at home" (Acts 5:42). While the community life of the church centered primarily in the home, worship and nurture took place both in the temple and in small house gatherings (Acts 2:42, 46-47; 4:34-35; 5:25, 42).[19] Although worship in the Jewish temple eventually ceased, both large- and small-group gatherings seem to have marked the common life of the early church throughout the Mediterranean world.[20]

These were the twin foci of early church life: the large congregation and the small group. This was also the pattern the disciples had followed with Jesus. For about three years the disciples spent much of their time either among outdoor crowds, in the temple or in private small-group conferences with the Master. There was always this small-group / large-group rhythm, the small group providing the intense community life which gave depth to the large-group gatherings.

Theologically, large- and small-group gatherings are the structural implications of the church's being the people of God and the fellowship of the Holy Spirit, as we have already seen. Peoplehood implies the necessity of large-group gatherings while community requires small-group structures. The threefold ecology of worship, community, and witness (chapter 10) also reinforces this structural implication.

Church history reveals a recurrent tendency to absolutize and institutionalize the large group, wedding it to a specific building and form, while neglecting or even condemning the small group. Virtually every major movement of spiritual renewal in the Christian church has been accompanied by a return to the small group and the proliferation of such groups in private homes for Bible study, prayer and discussion of the faith. Therefore, whatever other structures may be found useful, large-group and small-group structures should be fundamental. Although the specific form of such structures may vary according to culture and circumstances, both are necessary to sustain community and witness. No other structure or form should be allowed to subvert or replace either the large corporate group or the small fellowship group.

The large group and the small group are necessary not only for community and witness but also for discipline. Dean M. Kelley has emphasized in *Why Conservative Churches Are Growing* that discipline, or "strictness," marks virtually all significant and society-transforming religious movements. Says Kelley, "A group with evidence of social strength will proportionately show traits of strictness; a group with traits of leniency will proportionately show evidences of social weakness rather than strength."[21]

The gospel makes high demands of all believers and requires ardent discipline. But how is this discipline to be maintained? If the church is truly biblical, such discipline will not be imposed hierarchically but will be internal or intrinsic, enforced by the community itself on the basis of a fund of commonly shared values and under the leadership of the Holy Spirit. The small group is the natural structure for this function. It provides the essential context for instilling necessary discipline, for it is the place where common values are found, shared and reinforced. Not only is this sociologically valid, it squares with what Jesus and Paul teach (Mt. 18:15-20; 1 Cor. 5:3-13).

3. *A clear distinction should be made between the church and parachurch structures.* Christians must see themselves as the community of God's people, not in the first place as members of an organization. In many a contemporary church this would be revolutionary.

Each church should be helped to understand that institutional structures are legitimate (provided they really aid the church in its life and witness), but not sacred. The important thing, therefore, is not to prescribe which parachurch structures should or should not exist in the church, but to insist on the relativity and limitations of such structures.

4. *Churches should be part of an organic network.* This seems to be a fourth New Testament principle of church structure. Clearly no denominational structures are found in the Bible. Yet the Apostles maintained a functional, organic network among the churches. The Book of Acts shows this at a number of points, as do the epistles. The Apostles in Jerusalem felt responsibility for the new multi-ethnic church in Antioch, and sent Barnabas to check on it (Acts 11:22). The Apostle Paul maintained an active, effective network among the churches he founded for purposes of oversight, discipling, further evangelism, and mutual aid.

The New Testament says relatively little about this networking, so we should guard against concluding too much or too little. There is no biblical basis for hierarchical or pyramidal denominational structures (whatever their usefulness). Nor does the New Testament suggest the total independence of local congregations. We therefore should apply the organic, ecological principles of body life, recognizing a functional interdependence. "Submit to one another out of reverence for Christ" (Eph. 5:21 NIV) applies to churches as well as persons, for it is a biblical organic principle. The biblical pattern seems to be a functional, life-maintaining network of mutual accountability, recognizing and discerning the larger Body of Christ.

In summary, the church as the community of God's people should be structured on spiritual gifts of leadership and on some form of large-group and small-group gatherings, with a functional, nourishing inter-networking. Beyond this, the church should take care to distinguish between its essential self and all parachurch structures so that it does not become culture-bound, and so that, conversely, in periods of upheaval the wine is not thrown out with the wineskins. This is what happened, essentially, in Russia in 1917, and it could happen on a much wider scale in the future.

These principles are illustrated in figure 5.

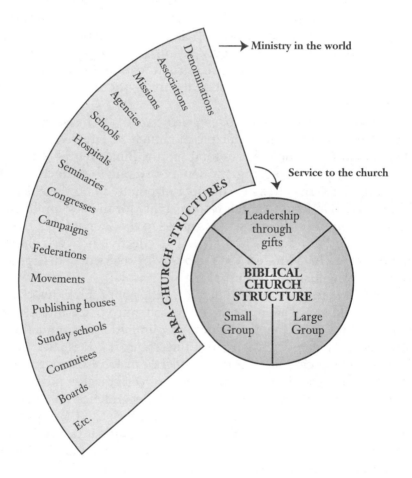

Figure 5. A Model for Church Structure

Implications for Cross-Cultural Witness

Several conclusions for the church's global, cross-cultural witness follow from the foregoing discussion:

1. *The church as biblically presented is always cross-culturally relevant.* This is true because the church is a cosmic-historical, charismatic organism that proceeds from divine action and transcends any particular cultural form. Since created by God, at its deepest level it corresponds to the structure of *what is*, the structure of reality as God made it.

2. *Similarly, the basic structures of charismatic leadership, small-group / large-group gatherings, and translocal networking are always cross-culturally viable.* This follows from the foregoing analysis and has also been abundantly demonstrated throughout church history and in the modern missionary age.

3. *On the other hand, parachurch structures are not always cross-culturally valid.* Since these are culturally determined, particular parachurch structures will be transferable from one culture to another only to the extent that the two cultures are compatible. Basic adaptations will often have to be made.

4. *The exercise of spiritual gifts will result in cross-cultural witness.* Since the beginning of the church and through the ages, God has been calling and sending out his charismatically-equipped missionaries. Paul related his own missionary ministry to the charismatic gift he had received (Eph. 3:7-8). The Antiochian pattern (Acts 13:1-4) has been repeated countless times and will continue to be repeated until Christ returns (Mt. 24:14). It is God who calls and who gives gifts, and the gift and the call go together.

5. *The church is itself a missionary structure, and any group of missionaries may be a legitimate embodiment of the church.* This means there can be no question of the church versus "missionary structures." Where missionaries are, there is the church. There missionaries are responsible to demonstrate the reality of Christian community. The real point of tension therefore is between the church as the community of God's people and institutional expressions of the church. If Christ is really in them, Christian witnesses can never go to another culture and leave the church behind. But they can, and often should, leave behind or modify the parachurch forms peculiar to their own culture.

6. *On the other hand, parachurch missionary/evangelistic structures should be created wherever necessary to get the job done.* While the church is God's agent for cosmic reconciliation, dynamic parachurch structures can be human agents of reconciliation. They can be useful in God's hands for the more rapid and effective spread of the kingdom.

Denominational groups should freely collaborate with other parachurch organizations that are doing work they themselves cannot do or that will help them carry on their own witness. Such organizations, however, should always be directed ultimately toward the formation and edification of the church (though in widely different ways) or the extension of the church's ministry, while not allowing themselves to be confused with the church or become ends in themselves.

7. *Since they are human creations and are culturally determined, all parachurch structures should be subjected to continuous, rigorous sociological and theological analysis to determine their fidelity to the biblical character of the church and their effectiveness as instruments of its mission.* We should not hesitate to make the most exacting sociological studies of mission agencies, evangelistic and relief organizations, denominational structures and so forth. Some parachurch structures should be devoted exclusively to this task.

History teaches us that many ecclesiastical structures will eventually succumb to institutionalism, becoming obstacles rather than helps to the church. The fact that God has raised up a movement is no warranty against eventual infidelity or self-centeredness. Having clearly distinguished such structures from the essence of the church, we can freely ask to what extent these forms are actually functional.

The better sort of such parachurch organizations will welcome this kind of evaluation and may even provide for it themselves (as some are now doing). Those parachurch groups which are nervous about such study are often the very ones most needing it.

There is no salvation outside the church unless the Body of Christ be decapitated, separated from the Head. For when one is regenerated he or she becomes a part of the Body of Christ. The church is the Body of Christ, the community of the Holy Spirit, the people of God. As such, it is the agent of God's plan for the reconciliation of all things in Jesus Christ.

The need of the hour is to understand the church as a Spirit-endowed charismatic organism which is cross-culturally valid, not as an institutional organization molded by the world. Once this distinction is made, the normal growth and witness of the church can be understood and planned for, and the various parachurch structures, including denominations, can be dealt with and used effectively.

A Lesson from History

DOES HISTORY OFFER any precedents for the vision of the church and church structure presented in the foregoing chapters? Where in space and time do we find a happy and vital union of gospel wine and church wineskins? Where has a clear gospel vision been coupled with viable structures to produce not only personal conversion but true community and cultural renewal as well?

I have already mentioned the radical wing of the Reformation and the movements that arose from it (chapter 3). These movements had great impact, but were unable to bring a thoroughgoing reform of both church and society. Many other examples from nearly every period of history could be cited and are worth studying.[1]

Carl F. H. Henry, in making "a plea for evangelical demonstration," cited two especially helpful historical precedents: the Wesleyan Revival in eighteenth-century England and the evangelical awakening in the Netherlands at the turn of this century under the leadership of Abraham Kuyper.[2] There are several good reasons for restudying both Wesley and Kuyper. Although standing in different Protestant traditions, both men were used by God for righteousness to such a marked degree that contemporary Christians ought to be asking *why*.

My own tradition places me closer to John Wesley, and I have been struck by the twentieth-century rediscovery of his abiding relevance. One can hardly pick up a book by an evangelical author without finding some reference to him. When contemporary writers wish to point out that evangelicals have historically had a social conscience, Wesley is cited. When the need for simple gospel preaching is stressed, Wesley is given as an example. The fact is that Wesley illustrates several qualities that are essential for Christian faithfulness in techno-urban society. I will survey these in this chapter.[3]

The Wesleyan Revival witnessed perhaps the most thorough-going transformation of a society by the gospel in history—a fact notably important for the modern church, since the Wesleyan Revival occurred during the period of upheaval that accompanied the Industrial Revolution in England.

It is probably true that the socio-political effects of the Wesleyan Revival have at times been overdrawn. The notion that Wesley saved England from a French-style political revolution is, at best, highly speculative and ignores important differences between French and English cultures of the eighteenth century.[4] Yet it is true that social conditions in England improved dramatically during the course of the century, and the Wesleyan Revival was a major factor in this change.

What is the relevance of John Wesley for the contemporary church? What were the factors that accounted for his impact?

Of the many which could be cited, six factors are especially relevant today. Three of these relate to Wesley's message and three to his method.

John Wesley's Message

John Wesley had a message, and he was not ashamed of it. He had something definite and specific to communicate, and the message was communicable in human language—a fact which needs emphasizing in our age. What were the principal elements of this message?

1. *A clear proclamation of personal salvation through Jesus Christ.* Wesley's message was salvation by faith. He emphasized the basic biblical teaching of human sin and lostness, Christ's sacrifice and resurrection, and the transformation of the new birth.

Some people said such a message was no longer relevant. People would not listen. But Wesley went on preaching, and the public response undermined the critics. People listened and responded by the thousands.

We must stress that Wesley's was a clear proclamation of the basic gospel. Though an Oxford scholar, he had no patience with high-sounding phrases that failed to communicate. It is said that Wesley would often preach newly prepared sermons to his maid, a simple, uneducated girl, and have her stop him whenever she did not understand his words. His passion was to communicate with the masses.[5]

This was the same Wesley who, preaching at Oxford, might quote from Latin authors or the Greek New Testament. Wesley was a scholar but he put his scholarship to work for the people.

2. *A consistent emphasis on the Spirit-filled life.* Wesley constantly stressed the need for the filling and continuing ministry of the Holy Spirit in the life of the believer, and thousands of early Methodists found the experience a reality. In nearly every city he visited, Wesley carefully examined the members of the Methodist societies about their Christian experience. Although he frequently found spiritual counterfeits, he also found much spiritual reality and power. The Holy Spirit was at work.

Wesley emphasized much more than merely a crisis experience of the infilling of the Spirit. His preoccupation was that of Paul: Christian maturity, building up the church, the forming of the stature of Christ in each believer. Wesley showed a constant concern for Christian nurture and growth through the work of the Spirit.

3. *An active and involved social consciousness.* Wesley was supremely an evangelist. And yet, read through a list of his sermon titles or of the pamphlets he published. His topics include wealth and economics, national sins, war, education, medical ethics, the Stamp Act, trade with North America, responsibility to the king, the liquor industry. He had a deep concern for social justice and national righteousness.

Everyone knew where Wesley stood on poverty and riches, sea piracy, smuggling, the slave trade and other hot issues of his day. Nor did he think he was compromising his call as an evangelist when he preached on these issues on Sunday morning. He saw, as had the Old Testament prophets, that biblical faith touches every area of life and makes every one morally responsible, from king to collier.

And the amazing thing is that Wesley's social concern brought results. Why? First, because he awakened a new moral consciousness in the nation. Second, because others followed his example. Third, because as an effective evangelist he was instrumental in transforming thousands of lives. He instilled in his converts the same social concern, thus broadening the popular base for social reform. He proved what the history of the church in other times and places shows: There is no combination more potent in transforming society than biblical evangelism coupled with biblical social concern—the joining of Old Testament prophet and New Testament evangelist.

Wesley himself did more than just talk about social reform. Among other things, he agitated for prison, liquor and labor reform; set up loan funds for the poor; campaigned against the slave trade and smuggling; opened a dispensary and gave medicines to the poor; worked to solve unemployment, sometimes setting up small businesses; and personally gave away considerable sums of money to persons in need.[6]

John Wesley's Method

But Wesley's message is only part of the story. He saw—or rather, learned—that the clearest, most biblical proclamation of the gospel often has little effect if it is locked within the walls (literal or figurative) of the institutional church. And it is here that Wesley becomes especially relevant for the problem of wineskins.

Others before and since have preached as clearly and effectively as Wesley, but with not half the abiding results. Why? In part because their message was encrusted in rigid unbiblical ideas about the nature of the church.

Wesley started out strictly "high church" in his ecclesiology, but God did not let him stay there. To a considerable degree he was still a high churchman at his death. He conserved the best of that tradition. But in many ways he learned to be remarkably flexible and unconventional. This can be illustrated by three aspects of Wesley's ministry.

1. *He did not confine himself to the institutional church.* The beginning of Wesley's effectiveness can be dated. It started when he began carrying the gospel outside the four walls of church buildings.

It happened like this: Wesley's friend, the evangelist George Whitefield, had gathered a large congregation of colliers (coal miners) at Kingswood, near Bristol. Here Whitefield preached regularly. This was "field preaching"—assembling a crowd in an open field or a town square and there opening the Word. Wesley frowned on this. He had been, in his words, "so tenacious of every point relating to decency and order that I should have thought the saving of souls *almost a sin* if it had not been done *in a church* [building]."[7] Whitefield requested—practically insisted—that Wesley take over his congregation so he could return to America. Wesley did not want to accept, but after seeing Whitefield's ministry, he felt the call was from God. So, "At four in the afternoon I submitted to 'be more vile,' and proclaimed in the highways the glad tidings of salvation, speaking from a little eminence in a ground adjoining to the city, to about three thousand people."[8]

The crowds grew, and soon there were congregations in other places—in fact, within a few years, throughout England, Scotland and Ireland. Wesley had discovered that when the people stop coming to the church, it is time for the church to go to the people.

Wesley, his brother Charles, and Whitefield did not win popular praise for their efforts. Bishop Leslie Marston notes, "These three men were called mad enthusiasts because they would free the gospel from the confining gothic arches of established religion and release it to the masses in street and field, to the sick and unclean in hovel and gutter, to the wretched and condemned in Bedlam and prison."[9]

Wesley was a devout churchman. He had no intention of founding a new dissenting group; he urged his hearers and new converts to attend the regular Anglican services. He never preached in field or marketplace at the same hour as stated worship services.

But Wesley was also a realist. He saw that many people simply would not attend the traditional church services. It meant entering an alien world. And even those who did attend failed to receive there the more personal spiritual help they needed. This leads us to the second aspect of Wesley's method.

2. He created new and workable structures for koinonia. One of the first things Wesley did was to divide the people who responded to his ministry into groups of a dozen, each group with its own leaders. These were the famous Wesleyan "class meetings." Wesley soon discovered the spiritual dynamic of this small group structure. He said in 1742,

I appointed several earnest and sensible men to meet me, to whom I showed the great difficulty I had long found of knowing the people who desired to be under my care. After much discourse, they all agreed there could be no better way to come to a sure, thorough knowledge of each person than to divide them into classes [or small groups], . . . under the inspection of those in whom I could most confide. This was the origin of our classes in London, for which I can never sufficiently praise God, the unspeakable usefulness of the institution having ever since been more and more manifest.[10]

We have already seen how Wesley later commented that through such small-group participation his followers "began to 'bear one another's burdens' and naturally to 'care for each other,'" coming to a deep personal experience of Christian fellowship.

Wesley innovated in other aspects of church structure as well—"lay" ministers (thus providing for the exercise of spiritual gifts), unpretentious "preaching houses" and so forth. He felt free to make such innovations because he saw Methodism not as a new denomination but merely as a "society" within the Anglican Church. Regardless of the reasons, he was one of the great innovators in church structure.

Wesley's efforts here say much to the contemporary church. Trapped in rigid institutional patterns, many of today's churches seldom experience that fellowship of the Holy Spirit pictured in the New Testament. This was also true of eighteenth-century Anglicanism—and Wesley did something about it.

3. *He preached the gospel to the poor.* One of the most crucial signs of the kingdom is to whom the gospel is being ministered. John Wesley, like Jesus, preached to the poor. He sought out those no one else was seeking.

Reading his *Journal*, one is struck with how many times Wesley preached at 5:00 a.m. or at midmorning in the marketplace. Why did he often preach at 5:00 o'clock? Not for his convenience, but for the convenience of the laboring men and women who went to work in mine or factory at daybreak. Wesley assembled the coal miners in the fields before they descended into the mines, or the crowds in the marketplace at midday. His passion was to preach the gospel to the poor, and there he had his greatest response.

In short, John Wesley had a message, and he did not muffle it behind stained glass. He went outside the structured church, preaching the gospel to the poor. He refused to allow newborn babes to die of spiritual malnutrition, but provided spiritual homes and foster parents for them. He created new forms of the church—new wineskins—for those who responded. He matched a biblical message with methods in harmony with a biblical ecclesiology.

John Wesley's Secret

Was there some special secret behind Wesley's impact? How did Wesley "happen" to find this happy marriage of message and method?

We face here at one level the mystery of the sovereignty of the Holy Spirit. But we can see at least some of the ways the Spirit worked in Wesley's life.

Wesley was not primarily a theologian, although he was theologically competent and informed. He "theologized" sufficiently to find biblical answers to the key questions of Christian experience and to confront social issues with biblical revelation. But he never tried to work out a complete theological system. His theology was a blend of high-church traditionalism, Continental Pietism, believers' church radicalism, and evangelistic pragmatism. On some questions, such as infant baptism, he never worked out a consistent position but held seemingly contradictory opinions (his way of mediating between Anglican tradition and biblical teaching).

There is not even unanimous agreement about whether Wesley was, at heart, an Arminian or a Calvinist! While he has generally been considered an Arminian because of his emphasis on a universal atonement and free grace, he was careful not to fall into antinomianism or universalism. Some have argued that his theology was really a variant of Calvinism.[11] If he cannot be neatly pigeon-holed, it is because he sought to be thoroughly biblical.

So Wesley's secret did not lie primarily in his theological attainments. It was not essentially theological in this sense. But it was essentially biblical. Wesley, the scholar, the author and editor of many books, was "a man of one book"—the Bible. He accepted it implicitly and practiced it consciously. This was his secret: the Word of God.

Wesley held the common-sense view that if the Bible is true, it will show itself true in human experience. So his points of reference were first the Bible, and, secondarily, experience, reason, and church tradition (the so-called "Wesleyan Quadrilateral"). These were his measures—but tradition, contemporary philosophy, and the opinions of others had to give way when they conflicted with Scripture, reasonably interpreted and experienced. What the Bible said was true, regardless of what the critics said, and would prove true in human living.

Because he was biblical, Wesley was free to be radical—radical in the proper sense of going back to the roots.

Not that Wesley was without his faults. Sometimes he sounded like an anti-catholic bigot, though his personal relations with individual Catholics were above reproach. Wesley was also a pro-monarchy political conservative with little patience for upstart American revolutionary radicals, though he sympathized with the colonists at first. Despite these or other criticisms, however, Wesley was at heart a Christian, as all who knew him well testified, and his faith was firmly, radically biblical.

Certainly Wesley had other things going for him besides those I have mentioned. He was a gifted administrator, discipler, and chooser of leaders (even though some of his chosen leaders later betrayed him). His editing, condensing and publishing of books— a complete library from history to medicine—was a ministry in itself. And he received immeasurable help from his brother Charles, who wrote thousands of singable hymns which were set to the popular music of the day. The early Methodists held an intelligible faith partly because they memorized so much of it in the hymns of Charles Wesley!

Each age is unique—but not totally. We can learn much from the past, and especially is this true with regard to the life and structure of the church. Few periods in the church's past shine as relevantly for today as Wesley's England. Here we find a useful model for testing the view of the church and church structure presented in these pages.

15

A Look to the Future

SOMEONE HAS SAID the problem of the present is that the future is not what it used to be. It's true! We are now living under the "pressure of the future" in a way that has never before been true during the history of our pilgrimage on planet Earth.

We live in a society that is qualitatively different from anything yet experienced by human personality. Although this time of ferment and transition shows marked similarities to the first-century Roman world, it is bringing the human race to a situation unprecedented in history. Human nature has not changed drastically, but human culture has evolved to the point where we find ourselves in a substantially different world. Needless to say, this fact has tremendous implications for the church and its structure.

Many are inclined to doubt that the world is fundamentally different today. Unconsciously reaching for stability, we prefer to think that society is not basically dissimilar from what it was in the past. It is merely more intense, moving more quickly. But the plain evidence reveals a more unsettling picture.

Alvin Toffler assembles an impressive array of fact and opinion in support of the uniqueness of contemporary culture in his books *Future Shock, The Third Wave,* and *Powershift.* Toffler points to "a growing body of reputable opinion [asserting] that the present movement represents nothing less than the second great divide in human history, comparable in magnitude only with that first great break in historic continuity, the shift from barbarism to civilization."[1] He cites economist Kenneth Boulding's comment that "as far as many statistical series related to mankind are concerned, the date that divides human history into two equal parts is well within living memory. . . . I was born in the middle of human history, to date, roughly. Almost as much has happened since I was born as happened before."[2]

The key facts here are the cumulative impact of technology and the resulting acceleration of change. What has happened within the lifetime of every person who will read this book is that the rate of change has so sky-rocketed that more change—and more *significant* change—takes place within one year than occurred in literally hundreds of previous years. And the rate continues to rise. This means that, unless there is a major catastrophe to stop the spiral, the few years between now and the year 2020 will see more change than has occurred since Abraham left Ur of the Chaldees. It will be as though all the political, scientific, industrial, social and religious revolutions of the past 4,000 years were crowded into one short lifetime.

An Accelerating World

Perhaps the two most eloquent symbols of our new age are the billboard and the TV commercial. Both tell us much about the kind of world we and our children will inhabit.

Both the billboard and the commercial are increasingly ubiquitous. Wherever we go we are bombarded by their messages. The images they project are nearly inescapable. This is symptomatic of the pervasive, invasive, dynamic culture being formed today. It is inescapable, as we see every time we travel along a busy expressway in Chicago, Seoul, or São Paulo. It is insistent. There is no "refuge from the world"; no private world any longer. It is not necessary for Big Brother to see us. It is sufficiently harassing for us always to see Big Brother and receive his messages! And today Big Brother is not the government or some political leader; he is computerized, nearly autonomous technology.

A second trait of the billboard and the commercial is their high degree of transience. Forty years ago a jingle or advertising slogan might last for years. But the rate of change has so sped up that now the advertising message, and even the product, lasts only a matter of months or even weeks. The impressive fact is accelerating transience. The billboard is not a permanent structure; it appears and disappears overnight. The message is printed on disposable plastic, for it is a disposable message. Today's "urgent" message is discarded tomorrow, replaced by another.

This transience is starkly typical of the new age, as Toffler and others remark. We increasingly think in terms of temporariness, not permanence. Within a year or two much in our lives changes—not merely familiar products, but our car, clothes, reading material and (for an increasing number of people) even our homes, friends, partners, jobs, associations and ideas. Contrast this with the lives of our grandparents.

Billboards and commercials have something else in common: sophistication. Huge amounts of money and talent go into advertising messages whose life is measured in only weeks of days. It is a joke that TV commercials are often more entertaining than the programs they sponsor, but this is a serious fact and only to be expected when one considers the money and sophisticated planning and analysis that go into every second of TV advertising or every square inch of a visual ad. Ben H. Bagdikian observes, "The most highly paid writers, actors, musicians, and producers in the world are not those that create education for the young, or drama for adults, or political programs for others. They are the men and women who create television commercials."[3]

Advertising is no laughing matter! It is, if anything, one of the most significant facts of the new technoculture, and increasingly so. It shows the shape of the future: society's greatest resources of money and talent being used to transmit a high-impact, high-transience, low-significance message in order to achieve a specific, predetermined result.

Which leads to another trait of the billboard and TV commercial: their high degree of manipulation. Not only is the advertising message predetermined; it is largely fictitious. The product hailed as "the favorite worldwide" really isn't. The service that subtly promises happiness really can't deliver. Advertised goods do not in fact provide what the advertisements promise. It would be pitifully naive, however, to suppose the ads are therefore ineffective. Quite the contrary! They achieve precisely what they are intended to achieve. They "create reality"—that is, an image—that predisposes a sizable number of people to respond as intended, normally to buy a particular product or use a particular service.

Political advertising at election time further extends this tendency toward manipulation and falsification. We have arrived at a high-tech society where planning and strategy mark nearly all areas of life, despite the hype about choice and freedom. People today are subjected to a dizzying number of messages—messages that have both great impact and little truth content. And these tendencies are rapidly accelerating.

These trends are significant in themselves. But I would call attention particularly to the direction they point and to the statement they make about the future—and what this suggests about faithful church structure.

When we look at the various crises of today—ecological, political, ideological, social, and economic—and then combine these with the fact of acceleration, only one conclusion seems possible: Time is running out. We must face squarely the fact that children being born today may be the last generation of humans to inhabit the planet—or else they will live on a planet that is hardly habitable, weighted and wracked by sickness of spirit, society, and environment.

Such a conclusion will sound absurd to many. Yet there is an impressive array of solid fact which, if not mixed with a rosy belief in progress and techno-fixes, points ominously in this direction.

Let us look at some of the evidence.

I have already mentioned the increasing transience and rate of change in society. The question is: Can the pace accelerate indefinitely? The famous historian Arnold Toynbee wrote back in 1966 that when we look at technology, "both progress and the acceleration of progress leap to the eye. At the present time, both are in full swing. Their impetus is unprecedented and portentous." Here we face "a new challenge—the greatest, perhaps, of any that have yet confronted" the human race. Though technology is a human invention, says Toynbee, "it is now challenging [our] ability to retain the power of planning, directing, and controlling [our] own future by the continuing exercise of the freedom of choice that is one of the distinctive characteristics of human nature." Created to serve us, "This inanimate apparatus . . . is now threatening to make a declaration of its independence of its inventor. It is threatening to carry [us] whither [we] would not."[4]

This fact of acceleration hits us wherever we turn. We are accustomed to seeing world population graphs shooting vertically off the page. But similar graphs could be drawn in many other areas—the information explosion, energy demand, urbanization, crime rates, the increase in basic scientific discoveries. Rapid acceleration in increasingly compressed time spans pushes the graphs steadily upward to the point where the line approaches the vertical. But when the graph line reaches the vertical, it must end. A crisis point arrives. Acceleration is not an infinite process; it is finite and eventually must stop—or else bring catastrophe. This is seen most clearly in population growth: Either it must slow down radically, or it will reach the catastrophe point where space, water, oxygen and food run out. And ultimately it makes little difference which runs out first.

Graphs are tricky, of course. Everything depends on scale. A slight increase can be made to look catastrophic, or a major jump can be reduced to a mere blip, depending on the how the lines are placed. We shouldn't be misled by graphs that seem to point to catastrophe, without digging deeper into the data. Even so, the underlying truth remains: History and change can't continue to accelerate infinitely. Some change must come: slow-down, renewal, or disaster. Which will it be?

Global society today is like a jet airplane, accelerating ever faster and faster. But there is a finite limit to how much speed that airplane can withstand. Unless it slows, it will eventually tear apart, disintegrating. It is not made to transcend the boundaries of space and time, and neither is human culture.

Satan's Final Strategy

Given this cultural configuration, the church today should be paying close attention to the Word of God.

Paul warns the church that "our struggle is not against enemies of blood and flesh, but against the rulers, against the authorities, against the cosmic powers of this present darkness, against the spiritual forces of evil in the heavenly places" (Eph. 6:12).

The battle to end all battles—literally—is on the horizon. And the enemy is not really communism or socialism or materialism; neither is it capitalism or imperialism or Big Government. It is subtler still.

The arch enemy is Satan, of course. But like vintage radio's Mr. Chameleon, Satan has a thousand faces. And the church today must be able to unmask him in his two most deceiving contemporary disguises.

191

The first disguise of the enemy is (for lack of a better term) *spiritism*. Some call it "spirituality," meaning something very different from authentic Christian discipleship. Involved here are astrology, the occult, non-Christian mysticism, virtual reality, and such anti-rational, subjectivist phenomena as drug-taking, humanistic meditation, and similar behavior. The common denominator here is a turning away from the real world, a turning inward to focus on one's own feelings, mind or inward state. The switch to the outside world is turned off; the inner world is switched on and becomes the only world that matters. As Timothy Leary put it, "Render unto Caesar everything material."

But is this demonic? Yes! Because it splits God's world into two irreconcilable parts, cutting the nerve between thought and action, between the subjective I and the objective world. It is deception because it fools a person into thinking that the only world that matters is what goes on inside one's own head or body or feelings. It cancels out the possibility of genuine Christian experience, which is both inward and outward. Worse yet, it plays into the hands of Satan's strategy for the last battle. Even sincere Christians fall into the trap when they focus so inwardly that they miss God's passion for redemptive living in the world.

The other Satanic disguise—only gradually and grudgingly coming to be recognized—is *technique*. This is the opposite of spiritism. It focuses only on the outside world, the observable reality. Its only ultimate concern is to find the best possible way to do a thing. But this becomes tyranny, for once the best way is found to build a car, elect a President, sell a product or obtain any other result, all other means are superfluous and doomed to extinction.

Today technique is building a society in which everything depends on technology. A complex technological pyramiding is happening in which ever more advanced technology is necessary to deal with society's problems. The realities of modern technology make ideology obsolete and focus attention on means, not ends. The important question is not Why? but How? What is technologically possible is therefore good. Technology replaces ideology, and esthetics becomes cosmetics.

But is this really Satanic? Yes! Because it cancels out all questions of ultimate purpose and meaning, putting all of life on the level of the "penultimate," the next-to-last. In the comfortable world of technique the fundamental questions of why and whither are forgotten. The future may promise a totalitarian technotopia not greatly different from Orwell's *1984* or Huxley's *Brave New World*. Such a possibility is anti-God because it becomes a God substitute and reduces human significance to the level of the machine.

The church's enemies today are spiritism and technique. Both enslave people, one by locking them inside their own experience (admittedly a wide world but only seemingly transcendent), the other by locking them into a comfortable, colorful, kaleidoscopic room with shrinking walls. In either case, there is finally no escape. Life is either experience without action or action without meaning.

But here comes Satan's dirty trick, and the meaning of the final battle: the marriage of Spiritism and Technique. It looks impossible, but it is happening. Technique is a "clockwork orange," a mechanical sponge. It absorbs everything and reduces culture to methodology, including spiritism and religion.

It is here that *1984* and *Brave New World* were prophetic. In both books a state-controlled, synthetic religion or religion substitute was provided to put meaning in life and keep all behavior within predictable and thus manageable limits. This insight is much more significant than the question of whether Orwell or Huxley were right or wrong in the details of their respective anti-utopias.

It is here also that the counterculture of the Seventies profoundly deluded itself. The serious drug-users, the communal drop-outs, the alternative consciousness children thought they were bringing a new revolution. They were deceived by the kiss of publicity into thinking they were succeeding. But the attention of the media was the kiss of death, and only the first step toward their absorption into the technological society. Behind the curtain one could hear the muffled sound of demonic laughter.

For in reality the anti-rational, the subjective, the experiential poses no threat to technique. The technological society is perfectly willing to make room for transcendental meditators or punk rockers, as Jacques Ellul had already pointed out.[5] For their introverted world is divorced from action and therefore not really revolutionary. It takes more than "consciousness" to bring off a revolution once technique has the upper hand. Such behavior is even welcome in technotopia, for it keeps the natives quiet, believing they are accomplishing something. Meanwhile computerized technique creates its own "virtual reality."

This is Satan's trick, and it suggests the shape of the church's last battle. What happened then to the old enemies of lust, greed, immorality, idolatry, sloth and so forth? They're still around. They're still demonic, and still fully employed. But the principalities and powers under Satan's dominion today are seen particularly in spiritism and technique, gradually merging into one demonic, seductive plan.

The Church Today and Tomorrow

What do these developments mean for the church—for both the wineskins and the wine?

1. *The whole question of church structure takes on increasing urgency.* As social acceleration increases, only those churches that are structured flexibly and biblically will be able to keep up. These churches will offer the best conditions for the church truly to be the messianic community in difficult days and to withstand persecution when it comes.

The church will increasingly have to choose between a charismatic and an institutional or bureaucratic model for its life and structure. Technological development, population growth, and other factors are speeding up the pace of change and squeezing humanity into a potential global ghetto. This acceleration of change puts new strains on all institutional structures.

Alvin Toffler argues that "the acceleration of change has reached so rapid a pace that even bureaucracy can no longer keep up." This means that "newer, . . . more instantly responsive forms of organization must characterize the future." We are seeing the "collapse of hierarchy" as "shortcuts that by-pass the hierarchy are increasingly employed" in all kinds of organizations. "The cumulative result of such small changes is a massive shift from vertical to lateral communication systems"—what John Naisbitt calls the megatrend from hierarchies to networking.[6]

Whether this is good or bad for the church depends on whether it is structured according to a charismatic or an institutional model. Biblically, it is clear that the church should be structured charismatically and organically, and any church so structured already is largely prepared to withstand future shock.

But churches that are encased in rigid, bureaucratic, institutional structures may soon find themselves trapped in culturally bound organizational forms which are fast becoming obsolete.[7]

A biblical conception of the church will make clear that the church is essential to the gospel, for it is the Body of Christ. At the same time, it will be clear that human institutions and structures are not themselves the church; they are not hallowed. But a biblical *concept* of the church is not enough. Local churches must *incarnate* the biblical reality by structures for worship, witness and common life such as we have been discussing in this book.

2. *The church must be watchful* (Mt. 24:42; 1 Thess. 5:6). These are days when Christians must be clear about what the church is and what it is not. Just as many false Christs will come in the last days, so many counterfeit and apostate "churches" will litter the spiritual landscape. We must not be led astray by our own fuzzy ideas of the church.

The church must be prepared, both as persons and as the Christian community, for the lash of persecution and the lure of the antichrist. This means the necessity for doctrinal clarity and authentic community—for both orthodoxy of belief and orthodoxy of community, to use Francis Schaeffer's phrase.[8] Under the threat of persecution, life in community becomes both more difficult and more essential. Thus the priority of structures which are flexible, mobile, inconspicuous, and not building-centered.

3. *The church of the future must be biblically sound and experientially authentic.* It must know a mysticism joined with action, profound experience wedded to practical exercise. The church must be a genuine community in which wholeness of life grows out of praise to God and fellowship with all people in Christ, without resort to demeaning techniques. The church must grow because of genuine spiritual magnetism, not by religious technology or contentless experience.

4. *The church must live and walk in the Spirit* (Gal. 5:16-26). It must learn in a deepening way the day-by-day guidance and direction of the Spirit of God. The Spirit must be free to produce the fruit and gifts which keep the church healthy and vital.

These are days in which the church must learn to "hang loose," to maintain its independence from the world and its dependence on the Spirit. Today's followers of Christ need to learn the full significance of the pattern of the children of Israel in the desert, who went or stopped when the cloud moved or stayed. They must learn to wait upon the Lord, to be sensitive to his leading and to depend less and less on the arm of flesh. Many local churches could benefit spiritually from applying the principle suggested by Robert Girard in *Brethren, Hang Loose:* "Anything in the church program that cannot be maintained without constant pastoral pressure on the people to be involved should be allowed to die a sure and natural death."[9] This is another way of saying that the church's life is to be based on the exercise of spiritual gifts, not on organizations and programs.

God in Christ has provided marvelous resources for the abundant Christian life. He gives us the strength to serve and endure. My prayer is that today's church will relearn what the early church knew: These resources are not just for the individual Christian. They are for the community, the church. May God grant that not only isolated believers but *the whole Body of Christ as a community and a people* may walk in the Spirit until it rises triumphant to meet Christ in the air.

In many ways, Christians today are reliving the New Testament age. These are days of rapid church growth in many places and yet also of spiritual lethargy, increasing apostasy, threatened persecution—and also expectation for the return of Christ. This was the situation of the early church. First-generation Christians thought Christ would come back. He didn't.

What about Christians at the close of the twentieth century? Like the first Christians, or like believers in 999 A.D., we could be mistaken about times and seasons. Perhaps Jesus' return is near, perhaps not. In any case, the church is clearly facing difficult days. Many believe that if Christ does not return soon, then some great catastrophe is surely coming.

But dare we hope for a miracle? Is it possible that God in his grace will grant another reprieve in human history, another chance for the church to really be the church? Is this the meaning of the Spirit's new stirrings in our day?

Is it possible that God yet has a great Kingdom task for the church to perform?

The church seems impotent before the ecological crisis, for example, or in the face of social unraveling or the worldwide web of political power and intrigue. But the weapons of our warfare are spiritual, not carnal. Using the world's weapons, the church does not stand a chance. But when the church uses God's weapons (Eph. 6:14-17), it is the world that grows weak.

These are not days for the church to turn inward, curl up in a corner and passively await the end. The world has yet to see what the Spirit can do through the church to establish God's kingdom on earth. God's "new thing" may have a greater beginning in human history today than we have thought possible.

In any case, these are days for extreme watchfulness: for alertness to what is happening in the world and for careful attention to God's Word to the church through the Scriptures. And these are days for great expectancy, for God's arm still is not shortened. He is still the God who says, "I will do marvels."

And it is the Lord Jesus who still says to the church: "Watch, therefore . . . ."

Postscript

Parable of the River

FROM HIGH MOUNTAIN reaches it came, coursing down rocky crags and between wooded slopes until it reached the plain. There it flowed, wide and quietly strong, its pearly surface reflecting the glory of the sun above.

The City was built beside the River. It was built, in fact, because of the River. For the people, the River was Life. Its pure water abundantly satisfied the City's thirst and watered its crops; it provided a variety of fish for food.

For many years the City lived on the banks of the River in pastoral tranquillity. The City grew and expanded. It built many houses and great public buildings. Along the River it built docks and parks and bridges. With time, the people found ways to harness the River's force, and built sluices and waterwheels and such. One idea led to another, and a whole culture grew up based on the River. There was prosperity and health for all.

Eventually the idea of the dam came up. The people had seen the River's power; they lived from it. How much more could be accomplished by a great dam, which would store the River's mighty power and give constant energy that didn't vary with the seasons.

And so they said, "Go to now, let us make a great dam to harness the River's power." And so they did.

It was a great project, and worthy. After some years the dam was done and brought new benefits to the whole City.

No one, however, perceived a certain problem. Though the City had harnessed the River, they had also changed it. As time passed, they had less and less of a River and more and more of a lake. And as the River's constant flow was impeded by the dam, its once-sparkling water changed to a murky hue. The change was so gradual, however, that no one really noticed. The glory and the benefits of the dam blinded the citizenry to less obvious but more sinister realities. Sometimes sickness and disease would come to the City, but no one connected these things with the changes in the River.

Meanwhile, something else was happening. The pure water kept flowing down from the mountain heights, and with time the level of the River gradually rose higher behind the dam. Then one spring as the snows began to melt on the mountains, the River started swelling to new levels.

Early one April morning the townspeople were awakened by a new sound. The thunder of rushing, roaring water clung over the City and echoed through the streets. City officials and all the people rushed to the River to see what was happening. The River was there, and the dam was there—but the water was rapidly flowing away. The dam had not broken, but on the far side of the River the earth had given way and a great gaping hole appeared. The River had broken through, and a foaming cascade of water surged and thundered through the breach. The water level began to recede, and the accumulated mud and filth of many years were swept away as the River poured forth in new power.

But consternation reigned in the City. The city officials called an assembly to determine what to do. Learned men reported on the situation and offered their theories. There were whispers of sabotage and subversion. Reports were heard that the River was now following a new course below the dam and surging across the plain, cutting a new channel.

There was, in fact, very little the city could do about the situation. But the City Council passed a series of resolutions. One condemned the whole lot of developments. Another forbade anyone in the City from going near the new River or drinking the water.

And so time passed. The city engineers were unable to close the breach or harness the new flow. So the City learned to live with it, as cities will do. Most of the people contented themselves with living their lives, taking care of the dam (now nearly useless), and with writing books to explain what had happened. Adjustments were made and life went back to normal.

But not so with all the people. There was, it is true, one small group of the poorer sort who thought differently. These strange ones said among themselves, "Why stay here by a useless dam and a sluggish River? Why not move on to the lower plain and build a new City along the River there? Is it not the same River?"

And so they did. The City Council did not approve. There were threats and accusations and more resolutions. But notwithstanding all this, a hearty group set out and followed the renewed River to the plain below, and there founded a New City. With time the New City grew and prospered, drawing its life from the River. Docks and parks and bridges were built. The people found ways to harness the River's force, and built sluices and waterwheels and such. One idea led to another, and a whole culture grew up based on the River. There were prosperity and health for all.

And then one day (a hundred years after the New City was founded, more or less) someone said, "Go to now, let us make a great dam . . . ."

Notes

Introduction

[1] Psalms 40:3; 96:1; 98:1; Ezekiel 11:19; 18:31; 36:36; Isaiah 62:2; 65:17; 66:22; Jeremiah 31:31; 2 Corinthians 5:17; Hebrews 9:15.

[2] The literature is extensive. See especially Alvaro Barreiro, *Basic Ecclesial Communities: The Evangelization of the Poor* (Maryknoll, NY: Orbis, 1982); Leonardo Boff, *Ecclesiogenesis: The Base Communities Reinvent the Church* (Maryknoll, NY: Orbis, 1986); Guillermo Cook, *The Expectation of the Poor: Latin American Base Ecclesial Communities in Protestant Perspective* (Maryknoll, NY: Orbis, 1985); James O'Halloran, *Signs of Hope: Developing Small Christian Communities* (Maryknoll, NY: Orbis, 1991); David Prior, *Parish Renewal at the Grassroots* (Grand Rapids, MI: Zondervan, 1987); Sergio Torres and John Eagleson, eds., *The Challenge of Basic Christian Communities* (Maryknoll, NY: Orbis, 1981). Prior's book applies the base community model to more traditional contexts.

[3] Useful sources are Robert and Julia Banks, *The Church Comes Home: A New Base for Community and Mission* (Sutherland, NSW, Australia: Albatross Books, 1989); Christian Smith, *Going to the Root: Nine Proposals for Radical Church Renewal* (Scottdale, PA: Herald Press, 1992); Lois Barrett, *Building the House Church* (Scottdale, PA: Herald Press, 1986); Bernard J. Lee and Michael A. Cowan, *Dangerous Memories: House Churches and Our American Story* (Kansas City, MO: Sheed and Ward, 1986); and Del Birkey, *The House Church: A Model for Renewing the Church* (Scottdale, PA: Herald Press, 1988). See also C. Kirk Hadaway, Stuart A. Wright and Francis M. DuBose, *Home Cell Groups and House Churches* (Nashville, TN: Broadman, 1987).

[4] See Ralph W. Neighbour, *Where Do We Go from Here? A Guidebook for the Cell Group Church* (Houston, TX: Touch Publications, 1990); William A. Beckham, *The Second Reformation: Reshaping the Church for the 21st Century* (Houston, TX: Touch Publications, 1995); and *CellChurch: A Magazine for the Second Reformation* (Box 19888, Houston, TX 77224).

[5] The key sources are Carl F. George, *Prepare Your Church for the Future* (Tarrytown, NY: Fleming H. Revell, 1991); Carl F. George with Warren Bird, *The Coming Church Revolution: Empowering Leaders for the Future* (Grand Rapids: Fleming H.

Revell, 1994); see also Lyle E. Schaller, *The Seven-Day-a-Week Church* (Nashville, TN: Abingdon Press, 1992) and Michael Slaughter, *Spiritual Entrepreneurs: 6 Principles for Risking Renewal* (Nashville, TN: Abingdon Press, 1995).

⁶ See, for example, Patrick Johnstone, *Operation World: The Day-by-Day Guide to Praying for the World*, 5th ed. (Grand Rapids, MI: Zondervan, 1993); C. Peter Wagner, Stephen Peters, and Mark Wilson, *Praying Through the 100 Gateway Cities of the 10/40 Window* (Seattle, WA: YWAM Publishing, 1995); Richard J. Foster, *Prayer: Finding the Heart's True Home* (New York: HarperCollins, 1992); Ted Haggard, *Primary Purpose* (Orlando, FL: Creation House, 1995), which represent different aspects of what seems to be a growing prayer movement.

⁷ On the Third Wave, see especially C. Peter Wagner, *The Third Wave of the Holy Spirit* (Ann Arbor, MI: Servant Publications, 1988), John Wimber, *Power Evangelism* (San Francisco, CA: Harper & Row Publishers, 1986), and John White, *When the Spirit Comes with Power* (Downers Grove, IL: InterVarsity Press, 1988).

Chapter 1

¹ As I shall later make clear, I am not depreciating theology or the necessity of a proper emphasis on truth. My point is that neither theology nor structures must be permitted to eclipse the Person of Christ and the new life he offers.

² Dietrich Bonhoeffer, *Letters and Papers from Prison*, rev. trans. (London: SCM Press, 1973). These comments of Bonhoeffer's are, at this point, merely suggestive. See especially chapters 4, 5, and 6 of this book.

Chapter 2

¹ I have given extensive analysis of today's global trends in my book, *EarthCurrents: The Struggle for the World's Soul* (Nashville, TN: Abingdon, 1995).

² Bonhoeffer, *Letters and Papers*, 188.

³ Ibid., 192.

⁴ Ibid., 200.

⁵ Ibid., 189.

⁶ E. M. Blaiklock, "Merely, Militantly Christian," *Christianity Today*, 15:16 (May 7, 1971), 6.

⁷ Herman Kahn and Anthony J. Wiener, *The Year 2000, A Framework for Speculation on the Next Thirty-Three Years* (London: Macmillan, 1968), 189. See also Snyder, *EarthCurrents: The Struggle for the World's Soul*, 132-36.

⁸ Ibid., 193.

⁹ Ibid., 7.

¹⁰ Adolf Harnack, *The Mission and Expansion of Christianity in the First Three Centuries* (New York: Harper Torchbooks, 1962), 19-22.

¹¹ Kenneth Scott Latourette, *A History of the Expansion of Christianity* (Grand Rapids: Zondervan, 1970). Vol. 1, *The First Five Centuries*, 73.

¹² Merrill C. Tenney, *New Testament Times* (Grand Rapids, MI: Eerdmans, 1966), 279.

¹³ *Cities & Slums News*, 1:4 (January-March, 1993), 4; Patrick Johnstone, *Operation World*, 35.

¹⁴ Quoted in Edward Krupat, *People in Cities: The Urban Environment and its Effects*

(New York: Cambridge University Press, 1987), 15.

[15] Harvey Cox, *The Secular City* (New York: Macmillan, 1965), 4.

[16] Will and Ariel Durant, *The Lessons of History* (New York: Simon and Schuster, 1968), 81.

[17] Michael Green, *Evangelism in the Early Church* (Grand Rapids: Eerdmans, 1970), 13-14.

[18] Noel P. Gist and Sylvia Fleis Fava, *Urban Society*, 5th ed. (New York: Thomas Y. Crowell, 1964), 23.

[19] Harnack, *The Mission and Expansion of Christianity*, 21.

[20] Ibid., 22-23.

[21] Zbigniew Brzezinski, *Between Two Ages: America's Role in the Technological Era* (New York: Viking Press, 1970), 111. ©1970 by Zbigniew Brzezinski. Reprinted by permission of the Viking Press.

[22] Latourette, 13.

[23] Green, *Evangelism in the Early Church*, 17.

[24] Os Guinness, *The American Hour: A Time of Reckoning and the Once and Future Role of Faith* (New York: The Free Press, 1993).

[25] Brzezinski, *Between Two Ages*, 64 (emphasis added).

[26] Green, *Evangelism in the Early Church*, 20-21.

[27] Ibid., 21.

[28] For example the *Time* cover story, "Astrology and the New Cult of the Occult," March 21, 1969.

[29] Latourette, 131.

[30] Cited in Page Smith, *Killing the Spirit: Higher Education in America* (New York: Viking Press, 1990), 3. For a fuller discussion of these issues see Snyder, *EarthCurrents*, especially chapter 15, "Postmodernism: The Death of Worldviews?"

[31] Harnack, *The Mission and Expansion of Christianity*, 1-18.

[32] Donald G. Bloesch, *Wellsprings of Renewal* (Grand Rapids: Eerdmans, 1974); David Stoll, *Is Latin America Turning Protestant? The Politics of Evangelical Growth* (Berkeley, CA: University of California Press, 1990).

[33] It is clear that Joel 2:28-32 was not totally fulfilled on the Day of Pentecost; not all the signs there indicated have yet occurred. As with many Old Testament prophecies, so here: There was an initial fulfillment (the "first installment") in the New Testament Age; there has been some continuing fulfillment throughout history by the Spirit's work through the church; and there will be a final complete and climactic fulfillment in the future. This final fulfillment is, of course, associated in Scripture with the return of Christ.

Chapter 3

[1] My convictions here arise from a careful study of the poor throughout Scripture (a study I was doing at about the same time Latin American liberation theologians began to write about God's "preferential option for the poor"), and also from my heritage in the Free Methodist Church, which was raised up "to preach the gospel to the poor."

[2] G. K. Chesteron, *The Everlasting Man* (San Francisco, CA: Ignatius Press, 1993), 205.

[3] John Calvin, *Commentary on a Harmony of the Evangelists, Matthew, Mark, and Luke* (Grand Rapids: Eerdmans, 1957), 2:36.

[4] Walter Rauschenbusch, *Christianity and the Social Crisis* (New York: Hodder and Stoughton, 1907), 82.

[5] Bruce Kendrick, *Come Out the Wilderness* (London: Fontana, 1966), 31.

[6] David L. McKenna, ed., *The Urban Crisis* (Grand Rapids: Zondervan, 1969), 138.

[7] Gibson Winter, *The Suburban Captivity of the Churches* (New York: Macmillan, 1962), 140.

[8] Ernest Campbell, *Christian Manifesto* (New York: Harper & Row, 1970), 9.

[9] Leighton Ford, *The Christian Persuader* (New York: Harper & Row, 1966), 152.

[10] Quoted in H. Richard Niebuhr, *The Social Sources of Denominationalism* (Cleveland: World, 1957), 29. See also Eric Hoffer, *The True Believer* (New York: Harper Row, 1966), 29-48.

[11] Ernst Troeltsch, *The Social Teaching of the Christian Churches*, trans. Olive Wyon (London: George Allen and Unwin, 1956), 1:39.

[12] John Wesley, *The Works of John Wesley* (Grand Rapids: Zondervan, n.d.), 3:445.

[13] Donald McGavran, *The Bridges of God* (New York: Friendship Press, 1955), 69-70.

[14] Donald McGavran, *Understanding Church Growth*, 3rd ed. (Grand Rapids: Eerdmans, 1990), 10-11.

[15] William R. Read, *New Patterns of Church Growth in Brazil* (Grand Rapids: Eerdmans, 1965), 225.

[16] Niebuhr, *The Social Sources of Denominationalism*, 54, 28.

[17] See especially Viv Grigg, *Companion to the Poor* (Monrovia, CA: MARC, 1991).

[18] Evangelism among the poor is complicated by the fact that the poor often represent one or more distinct subcultures within the dominant culture. Thus the problem of cross-cultural communication comes into play and must be considered. See, in this regard, Charles H. Kraft, "North America's Cultural Challenge," and Ralph D. Winter, "Existing Churches: Means or Ends?" both in *Christianity Today*, 16:8 (January 19, 1973), 6-8 and 10-13. The first step toward cross-cultural relevance, however, is the recovery of the biblical concept of the church. Lawrence Richards in *A New Face for the Church* (Grand Rapids, MI: Zondervan, 1970), 236-82, gives creative suggestions on ministering to the poor. See also Grigg, *Companion to the Poor*, and Robert C. Lithicum, *City of God, City of Satan: A Theology of the Urban Church* (Grand Rapids, MI: Zondervan, 1991).

[19] Niebuhr, *Social Sources of Denominationalism*, 34.

[20] Hendrick Hart, "The Institutional Church in Biblical Perspective: Cultus and Covenant," in *Will All the King's Men . . .* (Toronto: Wedge Publishing Foundation, 1972), 30.

[21] Donald Bloesch, *The Reform of the Church* (Grand Rapids, MI:Eerdmans, 1970), 113; John Howard Yoder, *The Fullness of Christ: Paul's Vision of Universal Ministry* (Elgin, IL: Brethren Press, 1987). While the reformers affirmed "the priesthood of all believers," they applied this emphasis mainly to soteriology (all may approach God directly) rather than ecclesiology (all believers are ministers in the church and priests to each other). See the discussion in Howard Snyder with Daniel Ruuyon, *The Divided Flame: Wesleyans and the Charismatic Movement* (Grand Rapids, MI: Zondervan, 1986).

²²Roland H. Bainton, *The Reformation of the Sixteenth Century* (Boston: Beacon Press, 1952), 95.

²³Niebuhr, *Social Sources of Denominationalism,* 39.

²⁴Bainton, *The Reformation of the Sixteenth Century,* 105.

²⁵There are several points of contact between the approach advocated in this book and the thinking of such groups as the Anabaptists, Quakers, and Plymouth Brethren (as well as similar groups elsewhere in the world). These groups took much of their original dynamic from their rediscovery of basic biblical truths about the church, though of course mixing these with other ideas and under-standings. Because of the historically conditioned nature of each of these groups— the "cultural factor"—no one of them (nor even the early church, for that matter) provides a perfect model for the church today. I am not proposing any historical group as an ideal model. Informed readers will discern that this book is not merely a restatement of views advocated by earlier reform movements. Rather, it is a call for serious reflection on the problem of church structure and for the fresh application of basic biblical concepts of the church to our age.

Chapter 4

¹Oscar Cullmann suggests that in John 2:12-22 the author "understands the clearing of the Temple as signifying that the *Temple worship* itself is replaced by the person of Christ." Christ himself is the center of worship; the temple has thus lost this centrality. Similarly, "When Jesus said after the destruction of the Temple he would raise up a Temple in 3 days (= in a short space of time) . . . it can only refer to the community of disciples." Oscar Cullmann, *Early Christian Worship* (London: SCM Press 1969), 72-73; cf. p. 117.

²"It is to be remembered . . . that if the work . . . and the history of [humans] are taken up by God and recapitulated in the glorified Christ, that is definitely not because they are valid, not because they make a positive contribution to improve that which God has willed, but because, in his love, God saves [men and women] *with* [their] works. It is by grace that he transforms evil into good, and wills indeed to take into account what [humankind] has done. The new creation is not superior to the first by the addition of [humanity's] work and history . . . , but by a new achievement of the love of God." Jacques Ellul, *False Presence of the Kingdom,* trans. C. Edward Hopkin (New York: Seabury Press, 1972), 29.

³The typological nature of the Davidic dynasty is particularly clear in God's promise that he would establish from David's line an eternal kingdom (2 Sam. 7:1-29 and 1 Chron. 17:10-27). Although there is a primary reference here to Solomon, the passage is clearly messianic.

⁴For example, in Micah 1:2; Habakkuk 2:20; Psalms 11:4, 18:6.

⁵On the Kingdom significance of the temple or house of God in Scripture, see my book, *A Kingdom Manifesto* (Downers Grove: InterVarsity Press, 1985), chapter three.

⁶A considerable literature exists arguing that the church should never own buildings; that any church that does so is unfaithful; and that the great fall of the church was its move from homes to church buildings. There is some truth in this view, but it is rather simplistic. Many other factors were at work; and

churches which shun special buildings can become as dead and cold as a petrified congregation meeting in a cathedral.

[7] But what about the Jewish synagogue? Wasn't It a building? Didn't the early Christians meet there? Wasn't it Paul's intent that the synagogues become centers of Christian worship?

The synagogue was in the first place a community of Jews; only secondarily did the term come to mean a building. There were hundreds of synagogue communities, as well as buildings, throughout the Roman Empire, and to these Paul went first with the gospel. Perhaps Paul would have liked to have seen these synagogue buildings converted into Christian centers, but, in the providence of God, that did not happen. The synagogues never became Christian church buildings, so far as we know, and within thirty years or so of the birth of the church the Christians found "the door into the synagogue . . . slammed in their faces" (Green, *Evangelism in the Early Church*, 195).

What Paul planted was not buildings—significantly, he built no physical synagogues; organized no building committees; appointed no trustees—but synagogue-like *communities*. As Ralph Winter notes, he "established brand new synagogue-type fellowships of believers as the basic unit of his missionary activity. The first structure in the New Testament scene is thus what is often called the *New Testament Church*. It was essentially built along Jewish synagogue lines, embracing the community of the faithful in any given place" (Ralph D. Winter, "The Two Structures of God's Redemptive Mission," *Missiology* 2:1 [January, 1974], 122).

It is interesting that the early Christians normally called themselves the *ecclesia* rather than the *synagogue*. Both Greek words can be translated *assembly* (cf. Jas. 2:2, where *assembly* in the Greek is *synagogue)*, and, grammatically, *synagogue* would have been an appropriate title for the church. The early church's preferences for *ecclesia* suggests a desire to clearly distinguish the Christian community from the Jewish synagogue. (See Harnack, *The Mission and Expansion of Christianity*, 407-08).

The synagogue provided a vital bridge for the gospel from Palestine to the rest of the Roman Empire and from Jews to Gentiles. But it was a bridge that, once crossed, was left behind. The early church copied the synagogue as *a pattern of community*, but apparently never *as a building*.

[8] John F. Havlik, *People-Centered Evangelism* (Nashville: Broadman Press, 1971), 47.

Chapter 5
[1] Walter Oetting, *The Church of the Catacombs* (St. Louis: Concordia, 1964), 25.
[2] It is true that there is a significant trend today toward greater flexibility in the construction of buildings. This is a positive sign. Where some form of physical facilities becomes necessary, high priority should be given to flexibility and multifunctionality. See Alvin Toffler, *Future Shock* (New York: Bantam, 1970), 55-63, 267.
[3] Lawrence Carter, *Can't You Here Me Calling?* (New York: Seabury Press 1969), 131.
[4] See chapter 7.
[5] In the first century, Christians often met in the private homes of people of

means who had been converted. Although by far the majority of Christians in the early church were poor, from the beginning there was also a scattering of wealthy converts. Their spacious homes often provided ample room for relatively large gatherings. Along this line, see Michael Green, *Evangelism in the Early Church,* especially 207-23, and Robert Banks, *Paul's Idea of Community,* rev. ed. (Peabody, MA: Hendrickson Publishers, 1994).

[6] Church groups I know of have met in schools, store fronts, shopping malls, community centers, and YMCA facilities. David Mains described one creative solution to this problem of a place for large-group worship in his book, *Full Circle.*

[7] Peter Wagner suggests that "the rule of thumb for churches that have been fired with a vision for a lost world in need of Christ is a minimum of 50 percent of the church budget for missions. They spend at least as much on reaching others for Christ as they spend on their own needs." C. Peter Wagner, *Stop the World, I Want to Get On* (Glendale, CA.: Regal, 1974), 66.

[8] Chuck Smith and Hugh Steven, *The Reproducers* (Glendale, CA: Regal, 1972), 55-63.

[9] Juan Carlos Ortiz, in an interview on July 19, 1974, during the International Congress on World Evangelization in Lausanne, Switzerland.

Chapter 7

[1] Keith Miller, *The Taste of New Wine* (Waco, TX: Word, 1965), 22.

[2] George A. Buttrick, ed., *The Interpreter's Bible* (New York: Abingdon Press, 1953), 10:425. Italics added.

[3] Hendrik Kraemer, *A Theology of the Laity* (Philadelphia: Westminster Press, 1958), 107.

[4] See Howard A. Snyder, *Models of the Kingdom* (Nashville, TN: Abingdon, 1991), 56-66.

[5] In my upbringing, the religious highpoint was the "altar service" which commonly followed the worship service if an "altar call" had been given and responded to. A few minutes to more than an hour might be spent singing and hearing the testimonies of those who had just found spiritual victory. Even though one can identify certain negative aspects to the traditional altar call and altar service, still (at least in my own experience) a deep if fleeting honesty, openness, and spiritual communion was tasted there which is unforgettable. That very reality further convinces me of the need for more viable and workable structures of common life which allow this reality to be experienced—not as an occasional "high" but as the normal life of the church.

[6] Robert Coleman, *The Master Plan of Evangelism* (Westwood, NJ.: Fleming H. Revell, 1963), 43.

[7] Though the Twelve were all men, Jesus also shared deep *koinonia* with a number of women, up to (and maybe a little beyond) the degree acceptable within the cultural context. The home of Mary, Martha, and Lazarus provided one opportunity for this; and Luke 8:2-3 and Mark 15:41 mention other women who shared this deep community with Jesus.

[8] Daniel J. Fleming, *Living as Comrades* (New York: Agricultural Missions, 1960), 19.

[9] I go into more detail about basic considerations for church structure in chapters

10 and 12 and in *The Community of the King* (Downers Grove, IL: InterVarsity Press, 1977).

[10] Quoted in Os Guinness, *The Dust of Death* (Downers Grove, IL: InterVarsity Press, 1973), 211.

[11] Robert Raines, *New Life in the Church* (New York: Harper & Row, 1961), 71.

[12] Banks, *Paul's Idea of Community*, 6-8.

[13] George W. Webber, *The Congregation in Mission* (New York: Abingdon Press, 1964), 81.

Chapter 8

[1] It may be that the statement "A man leaves his father and his mother and clings to his wife, and they become one flesh" (Gen. 2:24) implies an analogy to a people being called out from the nations to be one people for God.

[2] God still has a plan, of course, for the biological or ethnic Israel, for the Jews are still his people. In the end time the Jews and the church will be integrated into one faithful people of God (Rom. 11:1-36).

[3] Gerhard Kittel, ed., *Theological Dictionary of the New Testament*, trans. Geoffrey W. Bromiley (Grand Rapids: Eerdmans, 1967), 4:32.

[4] Ibid., 35.

[5] Ibid., 54.

[6] John Howard Yoder, *The Royal Priesthood*, ed. Michael G. Cartwright (Grand Rapids, MI: Eerdmans, 1994), 74.

[7] Ibid., 75.

[8] Jacques Ellul, *The Meaning of the City*, trans. Dennis Pardee (Grand Rapids: Eerdmans, 1970), 5-6, 77.

[9] Stanley Hauerwas and William H. Willimon, *Resident Aliens: Life in the Christian Colony* (Nashville, TN: Abingdon, 1989).

[10] See Snyder, *Liberating the Church*, chapter 10.

[11] Jess Moody, *A Drink at Joel's Place* (Waco, TX: Word, 1967), 22, 17.

[12] Yoder, 91.

[13] Is it possible there is a connection between the camp meeting movement and the social involvement of many nineteenth-century revivalists? I suspect there is, for the camp meeting provided a significant platform for social reformers and a large, sympathetic audience. See Timothy Smith, *Revivalism and Social Reform* (Nashville: Abingdon Press, 1957).

[14] For one attempt somewhat along this line, see H. R. Rookmaaker, *Modern Art and the Death of a Culture* (Downers Grove, IL: InterVarsity Press, 1970), 250-52.

Chapter 9

[1] Philip Morrison, "The Mind of the Machine," *Technology Review,* January, 1973, 17.

[2] Kittel, *Theological Dictionary of the New Testament*, 4:948-60. A good study of the biblical usage of *nous* is found in Mildred B. Wynkoop, *A Theology of Love* (Kansas City, MO: Beacon Hill Press of Kansas City, 1972), 132-35.

[3] Wynkoop, *A Theology of Love*, 121. See the discussion of Order, Surprise, and Beauty in Snyder, *EarthCurrents*, chapter 17.

[4] Kahn and Wiener, *The Year 2000*, 346-47. See Bertram Gross, *Friendly Fascism*

(New York: M. Evans and Co., 1980).

[5] Francis Schaeffer, *Pollution and the Death of Man: The Christian View of Ecology* (Wheaton, IL: Tyndale House, 1970), 47-50.

[6] Much of the problem with today's high-tech consumer society is the over-reliance on the "gross domestic product" (GDP) as a measure of economic health. The GDP simply measures economic activity, without regard for moral and non-quantifiable values. If we are going to use such an index, we at least need one that takes non-monetary values into consideration. See Clifford Cobb, Ted Halstead, and Jonathan Rowe, "If the GDP Is Up, Why Is America Down?" *The Atlantic Monthly*, 276:4 (October, 1995), 59-78.

[7] Toffler, *Future Shock*, 263ff.

[8] Snyder, *EarthCurrents*, 129-30.

[9] C. S. Lewis, *The Abolition of Man* (New York: Macmillan, 1947).

[10] Jacques Ellul, *To Will and To Do*, trans. C. Edward Hopkin (Philadelphia: Pilgrim Press, 1969), 185.

[11] Ibid., 190.

[12] B. F. Skinner, *Beyond Freedom and Dignity* (New York: Alfred A. Knopf, 1971), 102-03.

[13] Francis A. Schaeffer, *True Spirituality* (Wheaton, IL: Tyndale House, 1971), 112.

[14] George Orwell, *1984* (New York: New American Library, 1961), 47.

[15] The New International Version misleadingly mistranslates Romans 8:6-9, stating that Christians "are controlled not by the sinful nature but by the Spirit." The NRSV is more accurate: "You are not in the flesh; you are in the Spirit." The word "control" is not in the Greek original.

[16] Toffler, *Future Shock*, 263ff., 355ff.

[17] John Kenneth Galbraith, *The New Industrial State*, rev. ed. (New York: New American Library, 1971), 23, 53.

[18] Gary Henley, *The Quiet Revolution* (Carol Stream, IL: Creation House, 1970), 46-47.

Chapter 10

[1] The concept of "ecology" is based on the Greek word for house or household, *oikos*, a word (along with "economy," *oikonomia*), that has rich New Testament meaning. See chapter 2, "The Economy of God," in *Liberating the Church*.

[2] Biblical quotations in this chapter are from the New International Version unless otherwise noted.

[3] The church is sometimes described rather in terms of proclamation (*kerygma*), service (*diakonia*), and worship (*leitourgia*). Any conception of the church which does not see *koinonia* as basic, however, is a distortion of the New Testament picture. Also, I prefer *martyria* to *kerygma* as suggesting a more inclusive and incarnate conception of the church's witness, one which includes *diakonia*. On the tendency to overwork the idea of *kerygma*, see Green, *Evangelism in the Early Church*, 48. Heeding Green's caution that "it is all too easy to be beguiled by particular words into building a theological superstructure upon them which they were never designed to bear," I am suggesting worship, community, and witness as basic components not on the grounds of the technical use of these terms in Scripture but as general categories that cover the biblical revelation

and narrative about the church. Still, it is instructive to note some of the Greek counterparts to the English words and they way the three words are used in the New Testament. For a helpful brief discussion of *leitourgia* and the other New Testament words used for worship, see Ferdinand Hand, *The Worship of the Early Church*, trans. David E. Green (Philadelphia, PA: Fortress, 1973), 32-39.

[4] W. A. Visser't Hooft, *The Renewal of the Church* (London: SCM Press, 1956), 97.

[5] The incontrovertible biblical basis for this model is found in Ezekiel 10:10.

[6] See chapter 4, "The Church as Sacrament," in *Liberating the Church*.

[7] See the helpful discussions of the Christian year in Robert E. Webber, *The Majestic Tapestry* (Grand Rapids, MI: Zondervan, 1988). Webber has a very helpful section on worship which can serve as a healthy antidote to the shallowness of much contemporary worship and to what Webber calls "a kind of evangelical amnesia" concerning historic Christianity. On the other hand Webber does not, it seems to me, provide sufficient justification for taking second-century Christian worship as the primary model for worship today.

[8] Richard Foster, *Celebration of Discipline* (New York: Harper and Row, 1978), 1-9.

[9] In Scripture, justice and righteousness are closely linked, so that to speak of one is to involve the other. See the discussion in *Liberating the Church*, chapter 1, "Justice, Liberation and the Kingdom."

[10] See the fuller discussion in Snyder, *The Community of the King*, 107-16.

Chapter 11

[1] Paul Verghese, "A Sacramental Humanism," in Alan Geyer and Deen Peerman, eds., *Theological Crossings* (Grand Rapids, MI: Eerdmans, 1971), 137-45.

[2] Mains, *Full Circle*, 62.

[3] Ibid., 63.

[4] Elizabeth O'Connor, *Eighth Day of Creation* (Waco, TX: Word, 1971), 42-43.

[5] See, for example, C. Peter Wagner, *Frontiers in Missionary Strategy* (Chicago: Moody Press, 1971), and *Stop the World, I Want to Get On*.

Chapter 12

[1] On Pietism and Methodism, see Howard A. Snyder, *Signs of the Spirit: How God Reshapes the Church* (Grand Rapids, MI: Zondervan, 1989), especially chapters 3 and 5.

[2] Vinson Synan, *The Holiness-Pentecostal Movement* (Grand Rapids, MI: Eerdmans, 1971), 42. By 1891, "weekday meetings for the promotion of holiness," meeting mostly in homes and patterned after Phoebe Palmer's famous "Tuesday Meetings," numbered over 350.

[3] W. Stanford Reid, "The Grass-Roots Reformation," *Christianity Today*, 15:2 (October 23, 1970), 62-64.

[4] Elton Trueblood, *The Incendiary Fellowship* (New York: Harper & Row, 1967), 70.

[5] Raines, *New Life in the Church*, 70. The considerable success of the Disciple Bible Study program in the United Methodist Church, which relies on committed small groups, is another testimony to the same point.

[6] Moody, *A Drink at Joel's Place*, 24.

[7] George W. Webber, *God's Colony in Man's World* (New York: Abingdon, 1960).

[8] Webber, *The Congregation in Mission,* 21.

[9] Ibid.

[10] Webber, *God's Colony in Man's World,* 58-59. Italics added.

[11] Ibid., 58.

[12] Ibid.

[13] Webber, *The Congregation in Mission,* 131.

[14] Ibid., 122.

[15] Ibid., 82.

[16] Robert Coleman, *Dry Bones Can Live Again* (Old Tappan, NJ: Fleming H. Revell, 1969), 70.

[17] Webber, *The Congregation in Mission,* 163-64.

[18] Ibid.

[19] John Wesley, "A Plain Account of the People Called Methodists," *The Works of John Wesley,* ed. Frank Baker and Richard Heitzenrater (Nashville, TN: Abingdon Press, 1984-), 9:262.

Chapter 13

[1] Much of the content of this section is dealt with more extensively in *The Community of the King.*

[2] Donald A. McGavran, "The Dimensions of World Evangelization." Issue Strategy Paper prepared for the International Congress on World Evangelization, Lausanne, Switzerland, July 16-25, 1974.

[3] K. L. Schmidt comments that in trying "to understand the antithesis between an empirical Church and an ideal" in the post-apostolic church "there arises an awareness of the twofold nature of the Church as the Church militant and the Church triumphant. Such speculations introduce a distinctive ambiguity into statements concerning the Church. This is equally true of both the Greek and the Latin fathers. The greatest of them, Augustine, whose comprehensive thinking set the Church in the center of Roman Catholic life and thought, is the very one in whom the relation between the empirical and the ideal Church is not made clear. If genuinely Gnostic speculation was held at bay, speculation still established itself in the form of Platonism. . . . Protestantism, with its distinction between the invisible and the visible Church, has its own share in this unrealistic Platonism."

Schmidt says further that the church "as the assembly of God in Christ is not invisible on the one side and visible on the other. The Christian community, which as the individual congregation represents the whole body, is just as visible and corporeal as [an individual person.] . . . If Luther distinguished between the invisible and the visible Church, . . . he did so without accepting the Platonism of his successors." Kittel, *Theological Dictionary of the New Testament,* 3:533-34.

[4] I recognize there is a problem with the word *institution,* for any "established practice, law, or custom" may be considered an institution *(Webster's New Practical Dictionary).* In this sense baptism and the Lord's Supper, for instance, may be thought of as institutions, and it is difficult to make a distinction between *institution* and *church.* But I am here using institution in the more

restricted (and more popular) sense of "an established society or corporation"; in other words, as a formally structured organization, whether this structuring has come about by law, a constituting assembly or merely accumulated tradition. I am aware that some prefer to use the phrase *institutional church* to describe what I here refer to as community, but this is not the sense in which I am using the phrase.

[5] The same cosmic-historical perspective is evident throughout Scripture. All the promises of cosmic restoration in the Old Testament prophets apply here, reaching their climax in Isaiah. In the New Testament the essential message of the book of Revelation is the uniting of all things under the lordship of Christ. And Isaiah, Peter and John speak of a new heaven and a new earth (Isa. 65:17; 66:22; 2 Pet. 3:13; Rev. 21:1).

[6] Ephesians 1:10; 2 Corinthians 5:17-21; Romans 8:21. The Greek word "to unite" or "to gather up" in Ephesians 1:10 comes from the word for "head." The idea of Christ as the head of the church and of all things (for example, in Eph. 1:22) naturally suggests the thought of uniting all things under the headship of Christ. This accounts for Paul's using the rather uncommon word "to unite, to bring under proper headship" in Ephesians 1:10. See Kittel, *Theological Dictionary of the New Testament,* 3:681-82.

[7] 1 Corinthians 8:6, 15:28; Ephesians 1:22, 3:9, 4:10; Colossians 1:17-20; compare Hebrews 1:2-3, 2:8-10.

[8] For further elaboration, see Howard A. Snyder, *Models of the Kingdom* (Nashville, TN: Abingdon Press, 1991).

[9] Francis A. Schaeffer, *The God Who Is There,* 152; *Pollution and the Death of Man,* 66-69. See also George Elton Ladd, *Jesus and the Kingdom* (Waco, TX: Word, 1964) and Howard A. Snyder, *A Kingdom Manifesto* (Downers Grove, IL: InterVarsity Press, 1985).

[10] Peter Beyerhaus, "World Evangelization and the Kingdom of God." Biblical Foundation Paper prepared for the International Congress on World Evangelization, Lausanne, Switzerland, July 16-25, 1974.

[11] Clark H. Pinnock, "The New Pentecostalism: Reflections by a Well-Wisher," *Christianity Today,* 17:24 (September 14,1973), 6.

[12] Donald Bloesch, *The Reform of the Church* (Grand Rapids: Eerdmans, 1970), 112.

[13] Hans Küng, *Structures of the Church,* trans. Salvator Attanasio (London: Burns and Oates, 1964), 12.

[14] 1 Peter 4:10; compare Ephesians 3:10. In the Greek the word translated "manifold" *(poikilos)* often has the sense of "many-colored," as in the variety of colors in flowers or clothing. W. Robertson Nicoll, ed., *The Expositor's Greek Testament* (Grand Rapids: Eerdmans 1961), 3:309. See Snyder, *The Community of the King,* 61-63.

[15] Hans Küng similarly defines the church as "the People of God . . . the community of the faithful"; "the community of the new people of God called out and called together." *Structures of the Church,* x, 11. This definition is in harmony also with the etymological meaning of the New Testament word for church, *ekklesia*—a called-out and called-together assembly.

[16] This is the traditional Roman Catholic view, but many Protestant groups also

tend in this direction, with varying degrees of intensity and self-consciousness.

[17] That the functions of deacon, elder and bishop were associated with spiritual gifts is clear from such passages as Acts 20:28, 21:8; 1 Timothy 4:14; 1 Peter 5:1; 2 John 1. The *Didache* also suggests this connection between gifts and leadership functions.

[18] The ministry of the first "deacons" (Acts 8) and of Paul and Barnabas as missionary apostles (Acts 13:1-3) was recognized formally by the church; the evangelistic ministry of Philip and the apostolic ministry of Apollos seem to have become recognized informally as a result of their effectiveness. Note, however, that while Acts 8:1-6 refers to *diakonia* ("service" or "ministry"), the seven chosen are not actually called "deacons."

[19] See George Peters, *Saturation Evangelism* (Grand Rapids, MI: Zondervan, 1970), 33.

[20] Green, *Evangelism in the Early Church*, 194-222 and elsewhere.

[21] Dean M. Kelley, *Why Conservative Churches Are Growing* (New York: Harper & Row, 1972), 86.

Chapter 14

[1] There is an extensive literature here. A good popular survey is Thomas P. Rausch, *Radical Christian Communities* (Collegeville, MN: The Liturgical Press, 1990).

[2] Carl F. H. Henry, *A Plea for Evangelical Demonstration* (Grand Rapids, MI: Baker, 1971), 31.

[3] For more extensive treatment of Wesley and early Methodism, see Howard A. Snyder, *The Radical Wesley and Patterns for Church Renewal* (Downers Grove, IL: InterVarsity Press, 1980), and *Signs of the Spirit.*

[4] Maldwyn Edwards, *John Wesley and the Eighteenth Century* (London: Epworth Press, 1955), 82ff.

[5] In this and several other respects there are fascinating parallels between Wesley and another Oxford scholar, C. S. Lewis, a key figure in spiritual renewal 200 years after Wesley—though temperamentally Wesley and Lewis were far apart.

[6] Maldwyn Edwards gives an excellent summary of Wesley's efforts along this line in *John Wesley and the Eighteenth Century*. See also Mildred Wynkoop's *A Theology of Love*, 58-64.

[7] John Wesley, *Journal*, in *The Works of John Wesley*, ed. Baker and Heitzenrater, 19:46.

[8] Ibid.

[9] Leslie R. Marston, *From Age to Age a Living Witness, A Historical Interpretation of Free Methodism's First Century* (Winona Lake, IN: Light and Life Press, 1960), 66.

[10] Quoted in John Stott, *One People* (Downers Grove,IL: InterVarsity Press, 1968), 72-73.

[11] See, for example, the discussion in H. Richard Niebuhr, *The Kingdom of God in America* (New York: Harper Torchbooks, 1959), 205-06.

Chapter 15

[1] Alvin Toffler, *Future Shock*, 12.

[2] Ibid.

[3] Ben H. Bagdikian, *The Information Machines: Their Impact on Men and the Media* (New York: Harper & Row, 1971), 287.

[4] Arnold Toynbee, *Change and Habit: The Challenge of Our Time* (New York: Oxford University Press, 1966), 29.

[5] Jacques Ellul, *The Technological Society*, trans. John Wilkerson (New York: Alfred A. Knopf, 1970), 375ff.

[6] Toffler, *Future Shock*, 143, 139; John Naisbitt, *Megatrends* (New York: Warner Books, 1982, 1984), 211-29.

[7] Toffler (citing Max Weber) reminds us that bureaucracy, as an organizational form, appeared with the rise of industrialism, and suggests that it is passing away as many societies move into a post-industrial phase (*Future Shock*, 126). If this is true, it may be highly significant for denominational and other ecclesiastical organizations, and confirms a growing "post-denominational" phase for the church.

[8] Francis A. Schaeffer, *The Church Before the Watching World* (Downers Grove, IL: InterVarsity Press, 1971), 62.

[9] Robert C. Girard, *Brethren, Hang Loose!* (Grand Rapids: Zondervan, 1972), 73.

Index

Abraham, 93, 188
Acts, Book of, 29, 87f, 97, 121, 123f, 173
Adam, 93, 95
Advertising, 110, 122, 188ff
Africa, 32
Anabaptists, Anabaptism, 50f, 207
Antioch, 29, 173, 175
Apollos, 215
Apostles, 77, 91, 121, 144, 146, 171, 173
Architecture, 67-70, 89, 161
Argentina, 74
Ark of the Covenant, 58, 59
Astrology, 33, 192
Atonement, 55, 104, 106, 185
Augustine of Hippo, 213
Authority, cultural, 33

Bagdikian, Ben, 189, 215
Bainton, Roland, 50, 206f
Banks, Julia, 203
Banks, Robert, 203, 209
Baptism, 185
Baptists, 43f
Barnabas, 173, 215
Barreiro, Alvaro, 203
Barrett, Lois, 203
Base communities, 16f, 203
Beckham, William, 203
Bell, Daniel, 33
Beyerhaus, Peter, 166, 214
Bible, 91, 100f, 185f; as Book of the
    Covenant, 96, 101; in worship,
127f; study of, 91f, 132, 142, 149,
    151, 154f
Bird, Warren, 203
Birkey, Del, 203
Bishops, 171, 214
Blaiklock, E. M., 28, 204
Bloesch, Donald, 166, 205, 206, 214
Body of Christ, 18, 76ff, 84, 86, 98,
    104, 111-18, 123, 132, 137, 141f,
    162, 167, 173, 176, 195
Boff, Leonardo, 203
Bonhoeffer, Dietrich, 25f, 27, 85, 204
Book of Common Prayer, 129f
Boulding, Kenneth, 187f
Brazil, 33, 41, 44, 48, 98
Brzezinski, Zbigniew, 32, 33, 205
Buddhism, 33
Burma (Myanmar), 43
Buttrick, George A., 209
Byu, Ko Tha, 43

Caesar Augustus, 30
Cain, 95f
Calvary Chapel, 74
Calvin, John, 40, 206
Camp meetings, 100
Campbell, Ernest, 42, 206
Capitalism, 191
Carter, Lawrence, 67, 208
Cathedrals, 56, 72, 78
Celebration, 121ff, 125-29
Cell churches, 17, 35, 72, 100, 149, 203

217

Chambers, Oswald, 151
Change, social, 31, 187f; rate of, 188ff, 194
Charismatic Movement, 16, 17
Chesterton, G. K., 39, 205
China, 17, 30f, 35, 48
Christian year, 127f, 212
Church, 49ff, 118; as charismatic, 136f, 140, 146, 166ff, 177, 194; as organism, 18, 114-37, 177; as sign of Kingdom, 118, 166; biblical view of, 10f, 24f, 49f, 55-74, 78, 83-147, 161-68, 194f; congregational form, 50; early, 28-34, 43-47, 56, 64, 66ff, 76f, 87, 92, 121, 149, 196; ecology of, 117-37; images and models of, 18, 114-18, 162f, 182, 194; institutional, 23f, 35ff, 56, 83, 108, 113, 139f, 146, 151f, 162f, 168f, 182, 194, 214; presbyterian form, 50; purpose of, 118f; visible/invisible, 162, 213
Church buildings, 25, 37, 63-74, 150, 161, 168, 172, 183, 207f; symbolic meaning of, 66-69
Church growth, 16, 17, 24, 36, 47, 66, 124, 196; among the poor, 41, 43f; by division, 71f, 151
Church of England, 183f
Church planting, 25, 37
Church renewal, 16, 35, 136f, 147, 149
Church structure, 13-19, 24f, 37, 49ff, 76f, 88, 98-102, 111-15, 131, 161f, 194f; biblical principles, 169-74; flexibility, 71, 112f, 150, 194f; organic, 114, 136f, 169, 173, 194f
Cities, ministry in, 41-44, 48, 67, 153
Clergy/laity distinction, 50
Clough, John, 43f
Cobb, Clifford, 211
Coleman, Robert, 24, 87, 155, 209, 213
Colson, Charles, 24
Committees, 71
Communication, 89, 109, 151; mass, 31, 149, 151
Communion of saints, 86

Communism, 32, 191
Community, 24, 36, 49f, 67f, 73, 78, 83-92, 97, 104, 112ff, 119, 123-26, 130-37, 167f, 195; sacramental, 127
Computers, 35, 105ff, 110, 194
Comunidades de base, see Base communities
Conversion, 87, 95, 97, 104, 123, 142, 165, 179
Cook, Guillermo, 203
Corinthian letters, 76f, 84, 114, 117f, 140
Cosby, Gordon, 141
Counterculture, 193
Covenant, 55-58, 62, 96, 121, 130, 132f; celebrations of, 99f; New, 93f, 96, 168; renewal of, 100f
Cowan, Michael, 203
Cox, Harvey, 30, 33, 205
Creation, 142
Creativity, 139
Crime, 35, 191
Cullmann, Oscar, 207
Culture, 14, 24, 27-36, 96, 101, 113, 187-91; American, 30f; Greek, 30; in relation to church, 114f, 122, 135, 140f, 161-77, 207; renewal of, 179
CyberChurch, 18
Cyberspace, 153

David, King, 58, 60f, 63
De Mello, Manoel, 98
Deacons, 171, 214f
Denominations, denominationalism, 69, 98, 113, 155, 161f, 168-73, 176f
Descartes, René, 34
Discipleship, 17, 24, 48f, 51, 72, 108, 124, 130f, 192
Discipline, 125, 130ff, 172f
Doxology, 120, 127
Drama, 128
DuBose, Francis M., 203
Durant, Will and Ariel, 30, 205

Eagleson, John, 203

East Harlem Protestant Parish, 153
Ecology, 95, 190, 196, 211; of the
    church, 117-37
Economics, 181, 190, 211
Eden, Garden of, 95f
Edification, 123, 132, 167, 176, 181
Edwards, Maldwyn, 215
Elders, 171, 214
Elijah, Prophet, 93
Ellul, Jacques, 107f, 193, 207, 210,
    211, 216
Encouragement, encouraging, 131
England, 180ff
Entertainment, 122
Ephesians, Book of, 10, 46, 114, 118,
    133, 164f
Equality, ideal of, 32
Equipping for ministry, 113f, 156,
    171
Europe, Western, 107
Evangelicals, 36, 179
Evangelism, 16, 24f, 42-45, 47f, 68,
    71, 73f, 106, 113, 124f, 134-37,
    143f, 151, 165f
Eve, 93, 95
Experience, 106, 181, 192, 195
Ezekiel, Prophet, 61

Faith, 95, 111, 126, 128, 151, 180
Family, family life, 112; family as
    church, 112
Fasting, 132
Fava, Sylvia Fleis, 205
Fellowship, 46, 57, 67f, 83-92, 97,
    123f, 130f, 152, 184; see also
    Community, *koinonia.*
Festivals, 99f, 121
Fleming, Daniel J., 88, 209
Ford, Leighton, 206
Foster, Richard, 132, 204, 212
Free Methodist Church, 205
Freedom, 90, 104ff, 112f, 126, 190; of
    the Spirit, 90, 133
Future, 101, 126f, 165, 187-97, 205

Galbraith, John Kenneth, 110, 211

George, Carl F., 203
Gifts of the Spirit, 17, 49f, 76ff, 84,
    89, 125, 129f, 137-47, 149, 166f,
    171-75, 184, 195f, 214f; and
    abilities or talents, 142f; and
    community, 114, 133f, 139, 141,
    144; and the cross, 145f; con-
    sciousness of, 147
Girard, Robert, 196, 216
Gist, Noel P., 205
Gitlin, Todd, 34
God, nature of, 106; sovereignty of,
    95, 142, 145, 185; worship of,
    122f, 126-29
Grace, 95, 111, 118, 130, 133f, 141,
    144, 166, 185
Graham, Billy, 100
Green, Michael, 33, 205, 208f, 211, 215
Grigg, Viv, 206
Gross domestic product (GDP), 211
Guinness, Os, 33, 205, 210

Hadaway, C. Kirk, 203
Haggai, Prophet, 61f
Haggard, Ted, 204
Halstead, Ted, 211
Hand, Ferdinand, 212
Harnack, Adolf, 28f, 31, 33, 204f, 208
Hart, Hendrik, 49, 206
Hauerwas, Stanley, 210
Havlik, John, 64, 208
Healing, 77, 140, 143f, 146
Heaven, 56, 61, 87, 165
Hebrews, Book of, 55, 63f, 93, 131
Henley, Gary, 211
Henry, Carl F. H., 179, 215
Hierarchy, 171ff, 194
Hinduism, 33
History, 27ff, 126-29, 96f, 134, 163-66,
    168, 172, 176, 205; learning
    from, 179-86
Hoffer, Eric, 206
Holiness, 97f, 132, 212, as
    Christlikeness, 132
Holiness Movement, 149, 212
Holy City, 57

Holy Spirit, 17, 46, 48, 57, 63f, 77f, 83-92, 97, 105, 121, 123, 126ff, 132f, 135, 139-47, 150, 156, 181, 195f; "control" of, 110, 211; fruit of, 97, 132f, 195
Homes, importance of, 62, 87, 92, 121, 149, 154, 171, 208f
Homosexuality, 34
Hospitality, 144
House churches, 17, 18, 36, 66, 70, 171, 203; in China, 17, 36
Hutterites, 50
Huxley, Aldous, 193

Ideology, 32f, 130, 190, 192
Idolatry, 130, 194
Image of God, 103-09, 126, 132, 139
India, 43f
Individualism, 73, 88, 111, 124, 141f
Individuality, 105f, 111f
Industrial Revolution, 105, 180
Information explosion, 191
Institutionalism, 24f, 49, 56, 61, 83, 152, 155f, 161, 166f, 172, 176
Instruction, 125, 127; see Teaching
Internet, 18, 31, 33; Christian use of, 18
Irrationalism, 33f, 105
Isaiah, Prophet, 62, 129
Islam, 33
Israel, as God's people, 93f, 210

Japan, 33
Jeremiah, Prophet, 61, 142
Jerusalem, 71; destruction of, 56, 62
Jesus Christ, 55ff, 85-98, 101-06, 109-15, 118, 122-26, 135, 145f, 163, 171ff; as High Priest, 50; as sacrifice, 50; as Word, 101; fulfills tabernacle, 55ff, 63; incarnation, 100, 111; resurrection of, 96f, 100, 146, 168; return of, 166, 196, 205
Jesus Movement, 74
John the Baptist, 93
John, Apostle, 57, 93, 121

Johnstone, Patrick, 204
Judaism, 35
Judson, Adoniram, 43
Justice, 125, 129, 134f, 181, 212; and the poor, 38

Kahn, Herman, 28, 105, 204, 210
Kant, Immanuel, 27, 34
Kelley, Dean, 172, 215
Kendrick, Bruce, 40f, 206
Kingdom of God, 25, 41, 61f, 115, 124-27, 129f, 133f, 165f, 197; and creation, 115; in relation to church, 118, 126, 166; present and future, 165
Kittel, Gerhard, 210
Koinonia, 57, 67f, 83-92, 119f, 150-57, 168, 209, 211; structuring for, 89-92, 151f, 183f
Korea, 17, 33, 35, 99
Kraemer, Hendrik, 85, 209
Kraft, Charles, 206
Krupat, Edward, 205
Kuyper, Abraham, 179
Küng, Hans, 167, 214
Kwanglim Methodist Church, 99

Ladd, George Elton, 214
"laity," 94
Last Supper, 87, 96
Latin America, 16
Latourette, Kenneth Scott, 29, 32, 33, 204
Law, Mosaic, 55f
Leadership, 18, 75-79, 144, 151f, 171; charismatic, 171-75, 214f
Leary, Timothy, 192
Lee, Bernard J., 203
Legalism, 136, 164
Lewis, C. S., 211, 215
Liberation theology, 205
Lifestyle, 112
Lithicum, Robert, 206
Liturgy, 89, 90, 119, 126, 128f
Lord's Supper (Eucharist), 56, 121, 130; in early church, 121

Love, 45, 87, 90, 105, 108f, 118, 127, 130, 152; and spiritual gifts, 140, 145

Mains, David, 143f, 209, 212
Marriage, 112
Marston, Leslie R., 183, 215
Materialism, 25, 69, 126, 191
McGavran, Donald, 43f, 161f, 206, 213
McKenna, David, 41, 206
Megachurches, 17, 152
Mennonites, 50
Meta-church model, 17, 203f
Methodism, 99, 149, 156f, 179-86, 212, 215
Miller, Keith, 83f, 209
Mind of Christ, 103-15, 132
Ministry, 50, 133, 144; concept of, 75ff; of all believers, 17, 49, 55
Mission, 88, 94, 96, 134, 147, 149, 163, 175; church as, 175
Moody, Jess, 96f, 152, 210, 212
Morality, 106ff; decline of, 34f; technological, 107f
"Morphological fundamentalism," 83
Morrison, Philip, 210
Moses, 55-58, 63
Music, 121, 126f, 144
Mysticism, 23, 28f, 32f, 35, 86, 98, 109, 126, 162f, 192, 195
Mythology, 32

Naisbitt, John, 194, 216
Nationalism, 130
Neighbour, Ralph W., 203
Networking, 173ff, 194; and church structure, 173ff
New Age, 23
Niche marketing, "niching," 106
Nicoll, W. Robertson, 214
Niebuhr, H. Richard, 45, 49, 206, 207, 215

O'Connor, Elizabeth, 146, 212
O'Halloran, James, 203

Occultism, 192
Oetting, Walter, 66, 208
Ortiz, Juan Carlos, 74, 209
Orwell, George, 109, 193, 211

Palmer, Phoebe, 212
Parachurch structures, 168ff, 173-76
Pastors, 25, 75-79, 112, 144, 171; role of, 25f, 139
Paul, Apostle, 78, 84f, 93f, 97, 103, 114-18, 122, 127, 131, 141, 163f, 17ff, 191, 215
Peace, world, 30
Pentecost, 88, 100, 124, 128, 140, 168, 205
Pentecostalism, 17, 44, 98f, 150
People groups, 16, 36
People of God, 93-102, 123, 161, 167f, 172, 176
Personhood, 104f, 111ff, 114
Peter, Apostle, 78, 93f, 121, 163
Peters, George, 215
Peters, Stephen, 204
Philip, Evangelist, 215
Pietist Movement, 149, 185, 212
Piety, 132
Pilgrim people, 58f, 62-66, 95f
Pinnock, Clark, 166, 214
Plato, 34, 163, 213
Plymouth Brethren, 207
Politics, 110, 165, 188ff, 197
Poor, 32, 69, 130, 135, 205; and the Gospel, 17, 24f, 36, 37-51, 135, 181f, 184f; church planting and, 37, 206; in early church, 208f; in the OT, 37ff
Population explosion, 190f, 194
Postmodernism, 34
Power, 135; military, 130
Praise, 120ff, 124, 126, 134, 195
Prayer, 87, 89f, 121f, 132, 144,149f, 156
Prayer movement, 17, 204
Preaching, 84, 128f, 179f; outdoor, 182f
Priesthood, 55f, 64; church as, 93, 206

Priesthood of believers, see Ministry of all believers
Prior, David, 203
Progress, 107, 190
Promise Keepers, 17f
Propaganda, 110
Prophets, prophecy, 77, 140, 142ff, 146, 171, 205
Prosperity, 46
Protestantism, 49ff, 100, 162, 179, 214
Psalms, Book of, 100, 109, 127f
Psychology, 108f
Purity, 49, 132
Purpose, 109, 192

Quakers, 50, 207

Race, racism, 69, 151
Radical Reformation, the, 50, 179
Radical renewal, meaning of, 9, 25, 37ff, 44-49, 56, 130, 136f, 186
Raines, Robert, 90f, 151, 210, 212
Rausch, Thomas P., 215
Rauschenbusch, Walter, 40, 206
Read, William R., 44, 206
Reason, "escape" from, 33f
Reconciliation, 96f, 131; of all things, 164ff, 176
Reformation, the, 49f, 150
Reid, James, 85
Reid, W. Stanford, 212
Reissman, Leonard, 30
Relativism, 32-34
Religion, religions, 32f
Repentance, 100, 125, 129f
Revelation, 109, 127 see Word of God, Revelation, Book of, 57, 61, 128, 214
Revival, 36
Revivalism, 210
Richards, Lawrence, 152, 206
Righteousness, 135, 181, 212
Roman Catholic Church, 16, 36, 49, 162, 214
Roman Empire, 28-34, 56, 208
Rome, 29
Rookmaaker, H. R., 210

Rowe, Jonathan, 211
Runyon, Daniel, 206
Russia, 30

Sacraments, 127
Sacrifice, 55f, 62, 64, 121, 143, 146
Salvation, 49, 51, 86, 95, 167, 180f; personal and cosmic, 164f
Sanctification, 125, 130, 132f
Satan, strategy of, 191-94
Schaeffer, Francis, 106, 108, 195, 210, 211, 214, 216
Schaller, Lyle, 204
Schmidt, K. L., 213
Secularization, 27f, 128
Self-consciousness, 108f, 112
Self-control, 110, 211
Seminary education, 78
Septuagint, 94
Service, servanthood, 68, 84, 94, 97, 125, 134f, 144, 154, 196, 211, 215
Skinner, B. F., 108, 211
Slaughter, Michael, 204
Slaves, slavery, 29, 32, 38, 181
Small groups, 17, 47, 71f, 74, 91f, 101, 112, 114, 129, 131ff, 142, 171f, 183f, 212; advantages of, 150ff; as basic church structure, 149-57, 171f, 175; limitations of, 98
Smith, Christian, 203
Smith, Chuck, 74, 209
Smith, Page, 205
Smith, Timothy, 210
Social class, 45f, 69
Social reform, 182, 210
Social witness, 47f, 74, 181
Socialism, 191
Society, in relation to church, 114f, 122, 135, 144, 161ff; transformation of, 180
Solomon, King, 58, 60, 62ff
Songs, singing, 121, 127f, 186
Space and time, 87, 89, 91, 96, 98f, 163f, 166, 191
Spiritism, 33, 192ff
Spiritual gifts, see Gifts of the Spirit

Spontaneity, 104f, 112, 126, 140
Stephen, 63
Steven, Hugh, 74, 209
Stewardship, 46, 72, 132, 142; of
    gifts, 144
Stoll, David, 205
Stott, John, 215
Sunday school, 25, 68, 71, 78, 89
Synagogues, 208
Synan, Vinson, 212

Tabernacle, 55-61, 64, 66, 72f; con-
    trasted with Temple, 59ff
Teachers, teaching, 77, 84, 127f, 144,
    146, 171 see also Instruction
Technology, technique, 28, 30f, 35,
    104-10, 130, 153, 188, 190f, 192ff;
    and morality, 107f; behavioral,
    106, 108f; spiritual, 108
Television, 109, 122, 188ff
Temple, 55-64, 207
Tenney, Merrill C., 204
Tertullian, 43
Theology, 101, 109, 114, 204
Third Wave, 17, 204
Tithing, 38
Toffler, Alvin, 106, 187, 189, 194, 208,
    211, 215, 216
Tongues, gift of, 140, 143f
Torres, Sergio, 203
Toynbee, Arnold, 190, 215f
Tradition, 78, 113, 134, 156, 186
Travel, 31
Trinity, 87f, 117; as model of commu-
    nity, 87f
Troeltsch, Ernst, 43, 45, 206
Trueblood, Elton, 150, 212
Truth, 126f, 133, 204
Twelve-step groups, 149

United Methodist Church, 212
United Nations, 30
United States, 106f
Unity, 87, 104, 123; and diversity, 167
Urbanization, 27-30, 41, 48, 107,
    153, 191

Values, 34, 114, 122, 161
Verghese, Paul, 212
Vineyard Movement, 100
Virtual reality, 192, 194
Vision, 101
Visser 't Hooft, W. A., 123, 212
Vitality of church, 136f
Volition, 109f

Wagner, C. Peter, 204, 209, 212
War, 30
Watts, Alan, 89
Webber, George, 92, 152-56, 210, 212f
Webber, Robert E., 212
Weber, Max, 216
Wesley, Charles, 183, 186
Wesley, John, 43, 132, 149, 156f, 179-
    86, 206, 213, 215
White, John, 204
Whitefield, George, 182f
Wiener, Anthony, 28, 105, 204, 210
Willimon, William, 210
Wilson, Mark, 204
Wimber, John, 204
Winter, Gibson, 41, 206
Winter, Ralph, 206, 208
Witness, 84, 94, 96f, 119f, 124f, 133f,
    136f; cross-cultural, 175ff, 206;
    see also Social witness
Women, roles of, 32, 141, 209
Word of God, 101, 109, 111, 113, 127,
    185f, 191, 197
Worldviews, 27, 32-35, 107, 126f
Worship, 62, 67f, 70, 72, 86f, 90f, 119-
    30, 136f, 153f, 211f
Wright, Stuart A., 203
Wynkoop, Mildred, 104, 210

Yoder, John Howard, 94, 97, 206, 210
Yoido Full Gospel Church, 99

OTHER VALUABLE
CELL CHURCH RESOURCES

Where Do We Go From Here? By Ralph W. Neighbour, Jr.
"This may be the second-most important book you will ever read." Dive head-first into the vision for the cell-based church. Learn the overall structure and strategy of the cell church from a true pioneer. Find keys to successful basic Christian communities. Catch a vision for your church's future.

The Second Reformation By William A. Beckham
Bill Beckham's long-awaited book discussing the Two-Winged Church has arrived. He pours the foundation for this structure on the bedrock of the Bible, showing not only how the two wings are practical, but how they also reflect the very nature of God. For those already convinced of the Second Reformation cell structure, the closing section unfolds strategic plans for becoming a mature cell-based church.

Shepherd's Guidebook By Ralph W. Neighbour, Jr.
Dr. Neighbour draws from over 25 years of small group experience to paint the life of a cell group. What does it take to lead a cell group? Who makes up a cell? How large should they be and how do they grow? What do you do in a weekly meeting? Find answers to these questions and more and become an equipped cell leader. Includes 12 sample cell meeting agendas and forms to launch your journey.

Life In His Body: A Simple Guide to Active Cell Life By Dr. David Finnell
Key leaders and members must catch a personal vision for cell involvement. *Life In His Body* explains the cell vision in simple language and challenges the reader to personally commit to the essential elements of a successful cell church—prayer, community, evangelism, and leadership. Communicate the vision clearly to others with *Life In His Body.*

The TOUCH Equipping Track for Cell Members
TOUCH's vision is that every member of the Body of Christ be equipped to do the work of ministry. Though discipleship is inherently a spiritual thing, in order for Christians to be equipped there must be certain "spiritual stations" along the journey to maturity. Essentially, the equipping track seeks to balance the spiritual and the natural in the discipleship process. Each station is a handle both new and older Christians can grip as they grow spiritually and move along their personal "track." The equipping track is not meant to be a "magic disciple-machine" or a quick formula, but a model for intentional teaching, training, and sending—a model that has been tested and re-tested all over the world. Use it as a model for your equipping track in your unique situation.

Welcome to Your Changed Life begins the journey with a clarification of the life changing decision the new Christian has made. *The Journey Guide* gives the new cell member a simple understanding of where he is on his journey, and the commitment the cell has made to help him grow in the Lord. *The New Believer's Station* gives new Christians insight on listening to God, growing in His Word, Lordship and receiving Christ's freedom. *The Arrival Kit* brings foundational biblical principles to light, and includes a section especially for the sponsor. *The Sponsor's Guidebook* follows as station five. Cell members will find more spiritual growth comes through serving others as a sponsor, and this station tests their value system as they commit to discipling another. It gives practical handles for edifying another Christian. *The Touching Hearts Guidebook* includes 5 weeks of daily growth guides bringing the cell member through practical steps towards lifestyle evangelism and developing relationships with (Type A) unbelievers or the "man of peace". Station seven, *The Opening Hearts Trilogy* launches "share groups" to penetrate the world of the hard-core unbeliever. The last station, a parallel track entitled *Cover The Bible,* gives cell members a fascinating look at the entire Bible in a year. Listening to cassettes recorded in the pastor's voice, they will receive a bible college level survey of the Scriptures.

Cell Church Magazine
This quarterly resource for cell members and leadership provides current insights on this movement that is spreading across the world. Hear the testimonies of pastors who are on the road of cell church life. Gain practical information that is essential to life in the structure. Each issue contains a cell leader "toolkit" filled with problem solving techniques, testimonies of other cell leaders and ways to foster community, discipleship and evangelism.

Call TOUCH Outreach Ministries at 1-800-735-5865 if in the United States and 713-497-7901 if calling outside the U.S. for a free catalog on these and other TOUCH publications.